DEAR AMERICA,

Notes of an Undocumented Citizen

Jose Antonio Vargas

PRAISE FOR

DEAR AMERICA,

"An engaging read, and a deeply moving memoir of coming of age with the odds stacked against you and not only forging a remarkable life for yourself, but becoming a voice for transformation and cultural change." —*SAN FRANCISCO CHRONICLE*

"*Dear America* is a potent rejoinder to those who tell Vargas he's supposed to 'get in line' for citizenship, as if there were a line instead of a confounding jumble of vague statues and executive orders." —*NEW YORK TIMES*

"In *Dear America*, we get to know a young Vargas who was constantly told to stay in the shadows but whose tenacity and devotion had other plans for him."
—*LOS ANGELES MAGAZINE*

"Vargas writes with a newspaper reporter's spare, forceful prose, but he's searching and highly introspective." —*MOTHER JONES*

"This is a book for our times. Read it, feel it at a gut level, and go beyond the noise of hate politics." —**AMY TAN**, *New York Times* bestselling author of *The Joy Luck Club* and *Where the Past Begins*

"This riveting, courageous memoir ought to be mandatory reading for every American."
—**MICHELLE ALEXANDER**, *New York Times* bestselling author of *The New Jim Crow*

"One of the most important immigration rights activists of our time, Vargas has, in this brief book, brilliantly elucidated one of our major political issues."
—**HENRY LOUIS GATES, JR.**, Alphonse Fletcher University Professor at Harvard University

"This is a deeply personal and multilayered story told so gently and with such affection and humor that one hopes that it would convince even the most hardened nativist of the merits of the United States continuing to be what it has always been, a nation of eternal welcome."
—**DAVE EGGERS**, *New York Times* bestselling author of *What Is the What* and *The Monk of Mokha*

"Jose Antonio Vargas's powerful memoir is, among many things, a celebration of the millions of Americans who make immigrants like us feel at home in their country, regardless of our legal status, regardless of how much daily hostility we face. May this book cause their ranks to swell." —**IMBOLO MBUE**, *New York Times* bestselling author of *Behold the Dreamers*

Dear America

Dear America

NOTES OF AN UNDOCUMENTED CITIZEN

Jose Antonio Vargas

DEY ST.
An Imprint of WILLIAM MORROW

The author will donate a portion of his proceeds from *Dear America* to Define American, his nonprofit organization. For more information, visit DefineAmerican.com.

A hardcover edition of this book was published in 2018 by Dey Street, an imprint of William Morrow.

FIRST DEY STREET PAPERBACK EDITION PUBLISHED 2019.

Designed by Renata De Oliveira

The Library of Congress has catalogued a previous edition as follows:
Names: Vargas, Jose Antonio, author.
Title: Dear America : notes of an undocumented citizen / Jose Antonio Vargas.
Description: First edition. | New York, NY : Dey Street, [2018]
Identifiers: LCCN 2018031550 (print) | LCCN 2018041703 (ebook) | ISBN 9780062851369 (Ebook) | ISBN 9780062851352 | ISBN 9780062851352 (hardcover) | ISBN 9780062860972 (large print)
Subjects: LCSH: Vargas, Jose Antonio. | Journalists—United States—Biography. | Motion picture producers and directors—United States—Biography. | Illegal aliens—United States—Biography. | LCGFT: Autobiographies.
Classification: LCC PN4874.V37 (ebook) | LCC PN4874.V37 V37 2018 (print) | DDC 304.8/73—dc23
LC record available at https://lccn.loc.gov/2018031550

ISBN 978-0-06-285134-5 (pbk.)

21 22 23 LSC 20 19 18 17 16 15 14 13

To **Mama** in the Philippines,
and to every American who has made me
feel at home in the United States

To the world's migrant population,
258 million and counting

America is not a land of
one race or one class of men…
America is not bound by
geographical latitudes…
America is in the heart…

—CARLOS BULOSAN

Contents

Prologue xi

Note to Readers xv

PART I: LYING 1

1. Gamblers 3

2. The Wrong Country 7

3. Crittenden Middle School 11

4. Not Black, Not White 17

5. Filipinos 21

6. Mexican José and Filipino Jose 29

7. Fake 31

8. Coming Out 39

PART II: PASSING 45

1. Playing a Role 47

2. Mountain View High School 57

3. An Adopted Family 63

4. Breaking the Law 69

5. The Master Narrative 73

6. Ambition 81

7. White People 85

8. The *Washington Post* 89

9. Strangers 95

10. Bylines 97

11. Campaign 2008 103

12. Purgatory 105

13. Thirty 107

14. Facing Myself 111

15. Lawyers 115

16. Second Coming Out 117

17. Outlaw 121

18. Who Am I? 137

19. Inside Fox News 149

20. Public Person, Private Self 155

21. Progress 165

PART III: HIDING 175

1. My Government, Myself 177

2. Home 183

3. Distant Intimacy 187

4. Leaving 193

5. Staying 199

6. Detained 203

7. The Machine 207

8. National Security Threat 213

9. Alone 219

10. Interview 223

11. Cycle of Loss 227

12. Truth 229

Acknowledgments 231

Reading Group Guide 233

Prologue

I do not know where I will be when you read this book.

As I write this, a set of creased and folded papers sits on my desk, ten pages in all, issued to me by the Department of Homeland Security. "Warrant for Arrest of Alien," reads the top right corner of the first page.

These are my first legal American papers, the first time immigration officers acknowledged my presence after arresting, detaining, then releasing me in the summer of 2014. I've been instructed to carry these documents with me wherever I go.

These papers are what immigration lawyers call an NTA, short for "Notice to Appear." It's a charging document that the government can file with an immigration court to start a "removal proceeding." I don't know when the government will file my NTA and deport me from the country I consider home.

We are living through the most anti-immigrant era in modern American history. Immigration of any kind, legal or illegal, is under unprecedented attack. United States Citizenship and Immigration Services, which issues green cards and grants citizenship, has stopped characterizing America as "a nation of immigrants." To a degree unmatched by previous administrations, President Trump is closing America's doors to the world's refugees, slashing the number of refugees who can come to the U.S. by more than half. The everyday lives of "Dreamers," young undocumented immigrants who like me arrived in the country as children, are subject to the president's tweets. Trump conflates undocumented immigrants with violent MS-13 gang members, referring to us as "animals" and "snakes," often in front of boisterous crowds roaring with approval.

In a blunt warning to the country's estimated eleven million undocumented immigrants, Thomas Homan, acting director of Immigration and Customs Enforcement, told Congress: "If you are in this country illegally, and you committed a crime by entering this country, you should be uncomfortable, you should look over your shoulder, and you need to be worried."

Homan added: "No population is off the table."

A woman diagnosed with a brain tumor was picked up at a hospital in Fort Worth. A father in Los Angeles was arrested in front of his U.S. citizen daughter, whom he was driving to school. A young woman was apprehended after speaking at a news conference against immigration raids. A "zero tolerance" policy at the border rips families apart, denying asylum seekers their rights under international law. Toddlers are placed alone at "tender age" shelters, while parents struggle to locate their children. Every day, tens of thousands of people are jailed.

Since publicly declaring my undocumented status in 2011—greeted by the likes of Bill O'Reilly as "the most famous illegal in America"—I've visited countless cities and towns, in forty-eight states, engaging all kinds of people. Most Americans, I discovered, have no idea how the immigration system works, what the citizenship process requires, and how difficult, if not downright impossible, it is for undocumented people to "get legal." All the while, undocumented workers like me pay billions into a government that detains and deports us.

But this is not a book about the politics of immigration. This book—at its core—is not about immigration at all. This book is about homelessness, not in a traditional sense, but the unsettled, unmoored psychological state that undocumented immigrants like me find ourselves in. This book is about lying and being forced to lie to get by; about passing as an American and as a contributing citizen; about families, keeping them together and having to make new ones when you can't. This book is about constantly hiding from the government and, in the process, hiding from ourselves. This book is about what it means to not have a home.

After twenty-five years of living illegally in a country that does not consider me one of its own, this book is the closest thing I have to freedom.

Note to Readers

Mine is only one story, one of an estimated eleven million here in the United States. In the past seven years, I've met several hundred undocumented immigrants from all parts of the country, who greet me at coffee shops and grocery stores, approach me while I visited college campuses and spoke at events, and contact me through social media and email.

Although the details of our stories differ, the contours of our experience are much the same: Lying, Passing, and Hiding.

Dear America

PART I
Lying

1.

Gamblers

I come from a family of gamblers.

And my future, it turned out, was their biggest gamble.

Everything about the morning I left the Philippines was rushed, bordering on panic. I was barely awake when Mama snatched me from bed and hurried me into a cab. There was no time to brush my teeth, no time to shower.

A few months prior to that morning, Mama had told me the plan: We were going to America. I would be going first, then she would follow in a few months, maybe a year at most. Until that drive to the airport, Mama and I were inseparable. She didn't work, because I was her work. She made sure I was doing well at school. She cooked every meal: usually a fried egg with Spam for breakfast and, if I was good, her special spaghetti dish with chicken liver. On weekends, she dragged me to her card games and mah-jongg games. Our apartment was so tiny that we shared a bed. I was Mama's boy.

It was still dark outside when I arrived at Ninoy Aquino International Airport. For reasons she wouldn't explain, Mama couldn't come inside the terminal. Outside, Mama introduced me to a man she said was my uncle. In my ragtag family of blood relatives and lifelong acquaintances, everyone is either an uncle or an aunt.

After handing me a brown jacket with a MADE IN U.S.A. label in its collar—a Christmas gift from her parents in California, the grandparents I would soon be living with—Mama said matter-of-factly, *"Baka malamig doon."* ("It might be cold there.") It was the last thing I remember her saying. I don't remember giving her a hug. I don't remember giving her a kiss. There was no time for any of that. What I do remember was the excitement of riding in an airplane for the first time.

As the Continental Airlines flight left the tarmac, I peeked outside the window. I had heard that my native Philippines, a country of over seven thousand islands, was an archipelago. I didn't really understand what that meant until I saw the clusters of islands down below, surrounded by water. So much water, embracing so many islands, swallowing me up as the airplane soared through the sky.

Whenever I think of the country I left, I think of water. As the years and decades passed, as the gulf between Mama and me grew deeper and wider, I've avoided stepping into any body of water in the country that I now call my home: the Rio Grande in Texas, not too far from where I was arrested; Lake Michigan, which touches Wisconsin, Illinois, Indiana, and Michigan, states with big cities and small towns that I've visited in the past few years; and the Atlantic and Pacific Oceans—I'm the person who goes to Miami and Hawaii without ever going to the beach.

When people think of borders and walls, they usually

think of land. I think of water. It's painful to think that the same water that connects us all also divides us, dividing Mama and me.

I left the Philippines on August 1, 1993.

I was twelve years old.

2.

The Wrong Country

I thought I landed in the wrong country.

Filipino culture is fascinated with and shaped by Hollywood movies and beauty pageants. There were two television events that Mama and I watched live every year: the Academy Awards and the Miss Universe pageant. From an early age they shaped my vision of the world and of America. The America of my imagination was the America in *Pretty Woman, Sister Act,* and *Home Alone,* the America of Julia Roberts, Whoopi Goldberg, and Macaulay Culkin. The moment I landed at Los Angeles International Airport, I expected to see people who looked like Julia, Whoopi, and Macaulay—people who looked like the people I watched during the Oscars. Instead, I was greeted by something like the parade of nations that kicked off the annual Miss Universe pageant, with each contestant speaking in their own tongue. The America I first encountered at the airport was a polyphonic culture that looked like and sounded like what a bigger world was supposed to look and sound like.

In the Philippines, there were two types of weather: hot and really hot. Even when it was raining, even when typhoons knocked down trees and flooded homes, including ours, I don't ever remember feeling cold. The varied weather in California—warm and sunny in the day, cool and nippy at night—required instant adjustment. I learned how to layer my clothes, and I was introduced to a thing called a sweater. I owned jackets but had no sweaters.

The bigger adjustment was living with new people: my grandparents, whom I called Lolo (Grandpa) and Lola (Grandma), and my mother's younger brother, Rolan. Until Uncle Rolan moved to the U.S. in 1991, he lived with Mama and me. Lola had visited the Philippines twice, bringing bags of Snickers and M&M's and giving relatives and friends money (one-dollar bills, five-dollar bills, sometimes ten-dollar bills) like she was an ATM machine. If the word "generous" were manifested in one person, it would be Lola. I only knew Lolo from photographs, where he was always posing: back straight, stomach out, chin up, the posture of someone used to being watched. He posed in front of the house, in front of his red Toyota Camry, in front of some hotel in some town called Las Vegas. I was barely three years old when Lolo moved to America. By the time I arrived in Mountain View, California, Lolo had become a naturalized U.S. citizen. He legally changed his first name from Teofilo to Ted, after Ted Danson from *Cheers*.

To celebrate my arrival, Lolo organized a party that introduced me to all the relatives I'd only heard about but never met. There were so many of them it was like we had our own little village. Among the attendees were Florie, Rosie, and David—Lolo's siblings, whom I was instructed to call "Lolo" and "Lola" as a sign of respect. Filipinos like honorifics. Everyone older than you is either a *kuya* (if he's male) or an *ate* (if she's female). Unless they are a Lolo or a Lola, you call them Uncle or Auntie, even when you're not actually related. Lola Florie, in particular, commanded respect. Lola Florie, who worked in electronics, and Lolo Bernie, her husband, who served as a U.S. Marine, owned the house that we were living in. Their two American-born sons, Kuya Bernie and Kuya Gilbert, spoke very little Tagalog, yet still managed to instantly welcome me into the family. Lola Florie was the matriarch of the matriarchs in the family; she was the reason her older brother Ted and her younger sister Rosie had been able to come to America. Lola Rosie, the loudest and friendliest of my extended family, announced that Uncle Conrad had driven seven hours just to see me in person. Uncle Conrad was a legend in our family, having escaped a life of harvesting rice and doing construction work in the Philippines to becoming an officer in the United States Navy, a point of pride for all of us. Standing no taller than five foot three inches and speaking English with a gravelly, guttural Tagalog accent, Uncle Conrad was in charge of 92 enlisted personnel. He was Lolo's favorite.

"*Masayang masaya na kami na nandito ka na,*" Uncle Conrad said in front of the entire family as Lolo looked on. "We are very happy you are here."

To Lolo, America was something you wear, something you buy, something you eat, and he wanted to spoil his first and only grandson—me. It was consumption all around. In the Philippines, I got to eat ice cream only on my birthday, sometimes during Christmas dinner, and to ring in the New Year. I don't think I'd consumed as much ice cream in my entire life as I did in my first few weeks and months in America. To welcome me to my new home, Lolo's way of showing his love for me and showing off America was buying a tub of Neapolitan ice cream (vanilla, strawberry, and chocolate flavors, all rolled into one) for $5.99. I must have eaten a tub a week.

Another way that Lolo showed his affection was by printing my name, using a bold, black Sharpie, on every piece of clothing I wore, most of which were the T-shirts, shorts, pants, and underwear that Lolo and Lola had purchased before I even arrived.

"Ako ang nagdala sa iyo dito," Lolo told me on the day he signed me up for school. "I brought you here." He said it in a voice that emanated pure joy and familial ownership.

I didn't have a relationship with my father; I saw him no more than five times in my whole life. Shortly after I arrived in Mountain View, it was clear that Lolo would become the father figure I never had.

3.

Crittenden Middle School

"Oh, Jose, can you see?"

During my first weeks at my first American school, surrounded by my first American friends, I imagined my name was somehow in the national anthem, flashing a big smile whenever the whole class would sing "The Star-Spangled Banner."

"Hey," whispered my classmate Sharmand one morning when he caught me smiling while singing. "We're not talking about you." Sharmand sighed before saying, "The anthem goes, 'Oh, say, can you see.' You see?"

To say that I stood out at Crittenden Middle School is an understatement.

I wasn't fluent in English, and I stood out for my thick Tagalog accent. Tagalog, my native tongue, was not what anyone would describe as a soft language, at least not the way I speak it. My Tagalog was all hard consonants and chopped syllables with a quick, rat-a-tat-tat sound, like the sound of tropical rain pouring down on cement. Also, the Tagalog alphabet does not have "h" and "th" sounds, which meant I struggled pronouncing a very common word like "the." So "the" in English sounds like "da" in Tagalog, and whenever I said "da" instead of "the," I stood out. One morning, when Mrs. Mitchell, the homeroom teacher, asked me to read a passage from a book out loud during class, my classmates giggled when I said "o-tor" instead of "au-thor."

I stood out because of everything I did not know.

I didn't know what kind of food was appropriate to bring for lunch. I was the student who brought sticky rice and fried tilapia with a sauce while my classmates munched on food I'd never heard of, like peanut butter and jelly sandwiches. "What's that nasty smell?" my classmate Sharon asked. "It's called *patis*," I said. Fish sauce.

I didn't know how to play sports like flag football. The one time I did agree to play, I rushed to the wrong side of the field with the football in hand while my classmates, led by Sharmand, screamed, "You're going the wrong way! You're going the wrong way!"

I didn't know what *not* to talk about. When asked to talk about my favorite pet, I spoke about my dog Rambo, the only pet I ever had. I told my classmates that Rambo was named after the Sylvester Stallone movie series, and I said that the last time I saw Rambo was hours before Mama's birthday dinner, before Rambo was killed, adoboed (the popular Filipino version of stew), and served as *pulutan*—an appetizer. My classmates were mortified. A couple of them started to cry. I later explained that, in the Philippines, dogs can serve as pets and *pulutan*. (And, no, I did not take a bite of Rambo. I was too distraught.) When I was growing up in Pasig, part of the capital city of Manila, whose poverty-ridden slums house four million people, dogs and cats were fed what was considered leftover food—whatever was left from lunch or dinner, usually rice, bones from chicken, pork, or fish, skins from mangoes, bananas, guavas. I'd never heard of "pet food," never saw an aisle in a grocery store dedicated to food specifically for cats and dogs. One of my earliest memories in America was walking up and down the pet food aisle at Safeway, so transfixed and bewildered that I stopped one of the clerks. "Why does the dog food and the cat food cost more money than the people food?" I asked. The clerk answered with a long, hard glare.

America was like a class subject I'd never taken, and there was too much to learn, too much to study, too much to make sense of.

And I was excited to share everything with Mama. Long-distance phone calls were expensive. If I was lucky, I could talk to Mama once a week. Writing letters, first in longhand and later using computers at school, was cheaper. Writing letters to Mama was also a way to soothe us both, to ease the pain of our separation before we were reunited again. She was supposed to have followed me to America by now, but there was a delay in her paperwork. I had to wait some more.

On the first typewritten letter I sent Mama, written in my sixteenth month of living in America, I wrote:

What's up! How are you guys doin'? I hope all you guys are doing fine as well as I'm doing here with Lola, Lolo and Uncle Rolan. I just hate the weather here sometimes, it's too cold, I'm freezing! We even have to use the heater to keep us warm.

I wanted to show Mama that I was adapting to the language—the *what's up?–you guys–how are you doin'?* of it all. The first American student who ever spoke to me was Ryan Brown, his face covered with what I later learned were "freckles." When he greeted me by saying "What's up?" I responded, "The sky." I quickly realized that the English I spoke in the Philippines was not the same as American slang.

The letter continued:

> *It's really hard to be a 7th grader. It's like every week,*
> *we have a new project due! I'm getting crazy because my*
> *schedule is so tight. I go to school Mondays to Fridays*
> *from 7:58 a.m. to 2:24 p.m. I go to Tween Time*
> *Mondays to Fridays from 2:30-4:30. On Fridays, I*
> *go to Newsletter club until 4:30. I walk home, eat, on*
> *Tuesdays I take out the garbage and take a two hour*
> *nap and do my homework, I have plenty of homework!*
> *As usual I joined many school clubs like Tween Time,*
> *Drama, School newsletters. I think it's really so cool that*
> *I got to use a computers a lot. In the Philippines, I didn't*
> *even had a chance to touch a computer. Here in our*
> *school, computers are everywhere! Every room there is a*
> *computer. We can't write anything without a computer!*

Over time, America had become more than a class subject I was trying to ace. America was an entire experience, and I wanted to do all of it.

It'd been more than a year since Mama and I saw each other. I knew she was sad because I was sad. Anxious. The only way to make her happy was to make sure I didn't seem sad and to get good grades. Besides, I realized that being good at school—making friends, talking to teachers—was a way of blending in. Being accepted at school felt like being accepted in America.

> *Last quarter, I even got a Gold Honor Roll, I got 4.00, the perfect grade!*

As a single mother, Mama leaned on her closest friends, especially my godmother, for help. My godmother's family was a part of our family. Over time, as I got busier at school, it became more difficult to keep in touch with everyone. I tried.

> *I already wrote my daily life, how about you guys!? Are you all doing fine? Every night, I always pray that may all of you be in good health. I really miss all you guys! There is nothing more important than all of you! How's Ninang [godmother]? Is she doing fine? How about Ate Grace [my godmother's niece, who was like a sister to me]? I heard that she's graduating next year from high school. Does she have a boyfriend now? I hope not. Tell her to please write me. How about Tita Josie [my godmother's sister], Tita Nancy [my godmother's other sister] and Lola Elvie [my godmother's mother]? Tell them that I miss all of them and tell them that I won't ever forget them!*
>
> *Gotta go! I love all you very, very, very, very much!*

Mama recently mailed me this letter, which I sent her more than twenty-three years ago. As I read it now, I don't recognize that young boy. What happened to all that love and longing I felt for the family and friends I'd left? Separation not only divides families; separation buries emotion, buries it so far down you can't touch it. I don't think I would ever love Mama again in the childlike, carefree, innocent way I loved her while writing that letter. I don't know where that young boy went.

4.

Not Black, Not White

"You don't really look Filipino," Eleanor, the pretty girl in glasses and pigtails, was telling me. Born in the Philippines, Eleanor's family emigrated to the U.S. around the same time my family did.

Our arrival in Mountain View coincided with a historic change in the state's demographics. Between 1990 and 2000, the years I attended California public schools, the state's Latino and Asian populations each grew by more than a third. Meanwhile, the state's white population dropped by almost 10 percent and the black population more or less stayed the same—a statewide trend that would closely mirror the country's racial makeup in the following decades.

Crittenden Middle School was a microcosm of this irreversible movement. Like California itself, Crittenden was a minority-majority school where no single racial group had a plurality. In the early to mid-1990s, between thirteen hundred and fourteen hundred students from fifth to eighth grade attended Crittenden. About a third were Latinos, mostly Mexican; the other third were Asians, most of whom were Filipino, some Vietnamese and Indian; and the remaining third were split between white and black students. Many of the Mexicans and Filipinos were descendants of farmworkers who moved to Mountain View to work on the apricot, peach, and cherry orchards after World War II. A decade later, a Mountain View–based company called Shockley Semiconductor Laboratory first developed the silicon semiconductor devices that gave Silicon Valley its name.

Like many Filipinos in the Philippines, I grew up listening to Michael Jackson and Whitney Houston, but I didn't know Whitney and Michael were "black" or "African American." And I didn't know that Julia Roberts and Macaulay Culkin were "white." In the Philippines they were just Americans.

When it came to the subject of race, my fourteen-year-old immigrant brain couldn't process it. I knew I was Filipino; that much was clear. But I didn't realize I was "Asian," or that Chinese and Korean and Indian people were "Asian," too, and that because I was Filipino, I was both "Asian" and a "Pacific Islander." Calling people "Hispanic" or "Latino" was perplexing to me, partly due to the fact that people assumed I was Hispanic or Latino because of my name. (My stock answer: "My name is Jose because of Spanish colonialism.") Are people labeled "Asian" for geographic reasons, because we came from the "Asian" continent? But, if it was about geography, shouldn't "Hispanic" and "Latino" people be called "Americans"? According to the maps—and to the Miss Universe pageants that I watched religiously as a kid—"Hispanic" and "Latino" people were from Central and South America. What was the difference among these Americas? People come from the Philippines, from Mexico, from Egypt, from France. As far as I could tell, "white" was not a country. Neither was "black." I looked at the maps. Are people "Asian" and "His-panic" because Americans started labeling people "black" and "white"? Did America make all of this up? And whenever I read anything about race, why are "Asian" and "Hispanic" capitalized while "black" and "white" are not? Where do you go if you are multiracial and multiethnic?

I'll never forget the day of the O. J. Simpson verdict. I had no idea who Simpson was. But most of my classmates seemed to know, and most everyone had an opinion on what he did and why he did it, including my teachers, all of whom were white. On the day of the verdict, Mrs. Wakefield, who taught social studies, stopped the class and turned on the radio so everyone could listen. When Simpson was acquitted, the school erupted, the reaction spilling from the classrooms into the quad. It was the first time I saw race physically divide people. Black students cheered the outcome, white students jeered it, and Latino and Asian students—who made up more half the school—looked at each other, wondering which side to join. This dynamic—Latinos and Asians seemingly left out of the black-and-white binary—would become a dominant question in my life. Where do I go? Do I go black? Do I go white? Can I do both?

"You're not black, you're not white," Mrs. Wakefield told me during one of our afternoon chats. An elderly white woman, she walked around campus with chalk all over her hair, with oversize eyes that could see more than what you were willing to share. Mrs. Wakefield was the first teacher I developed a friendship with.

"Consider yourself lucky."

I didn't. I was just mystified. But what was becoming

clear—and what I started internalizing during my years at Crittenden—was that race was a tangible, torturous, black-or-white thing in a country where conversations about how you identify and whom you represent largely fall into two extremes. Nonblack, nonwhite people had to figure out which side they fell on and to which degree.

In my early formative days in America, while observing my classmates and watching TV and movies, I learned that race was as much about behavior—perceived behavior, expected behavior—as it was about physicality. "Don't be too white," I overheard my Mexican classmates tell each other. "Why are you acting so black?" my Filipino friends said to one another. None of the comments sounded complimentary. Sometimes the comments from my nonwhite, nonblack classmates were as negative toward "white" people as they were toward "black" people. Too often I stayed silent because I didn't know what to say.

I wasn't sure how a Filipino was supposed to look, or where a Filipino was supposed to fit.

5.

Filipinos

Filipinos fit everywhere and nowhere at all.

We are the invisible of the invisibles, a staggering feat considering that the worldwide Filipino population stands at 115 million: about 105 million live in the Philippine islands (making the Philippines the world's twelfth-most-populous country, just below Mexico); and an additional ten million are scattered across a hundred countries, most whom are permanent legal residents or citizens of one of those countries. Of the ten million overseas Filipinos, more than 3.5 million live in the U.S., making us the second-largest Asian group in the U.S. Even though one out of five Asian Americans is Filipino, many of us don't identify as Asian. Our Filipinotowns aren't as visible as Koreatowns and Chinatowns. Wherever we are and however we self-identify, non-Filipinos have an interesting way of identifying us. Even though our jobs are as varied as our people—we're nurses and lawyers, artists and professors—most people I meet seem to think of us as servants. Apparently, we are among the most sought-after group of domestic workers. I've lost count of how many times someone told me, apropos of nothing, "You guys make the best nannies and maids."

Perhaps that's because Filipino culture, while proud of its singularity and eccentricity, is so malleable. Adaptability was essential for surviving 420 years of emotional and physical ravages.

A colonial history, in brief: The Philippine islands were "discovered" by Spanish colonialists who ruled them for more than 370 years until the Americans, desperate to expand their economic and political reach, craved empire. The United States declared itself the rightful "owner" of the islands for some fifty years. In his book *In Our Image: America's Empire in the Philippines,* historian Stanley Karnow characterized my birth country's colonial history as being "300 years in the convent, 50 years in Hollywood." My grandparents embodied this unshakable colonial-imperial reality. Both devout Catholics—the Philippines is the only predominantly Catholic country in Asia—Lolo learned English words and phrases by listening to Frank Sinatra and Dean Martin in jukeboxes, while Lola preferred Nat King Cole and Ella Fitzgerald.

Some of my Filipino American friends joke that Americans only remember Filipinos when they need us to house their naval fleet and fight their battles. Consider the fate of Filipino soldiers who fought the Japanese during World War II. With the promise of U.S. citizenship and full veteran benefits, more than 250,000 Filipino soldiers fought under the American flag, playing a crucial role in achieving victory. Shortly after, the Rescission Act of 1946 retroactively took away these soldiers' status as U.S. veterans. The message was clear: your service didn't matter. It took more than sixty years to rectify the injustice.

From the outset, this codependent and abusive relationship has been complicated by race and skin color. During the Philippine-American War, white American soldiers in the Philippines referred to Filipinos as "niggers" because of their dark complexion. When Filipinos first arrived in California, in the early to mid-1900s, confused Americans placed them in the same ethnic category as Mongolians. In California, local authorities imposed antimiscegenation laws on Filipinos, and Filipinos had to drive out of state in order to marry white women. Throughout the Great Depression, white Americans claimed that Filipinos "brought down the standard of living because they worked for low wages." Many hotels, restaurants, and even swimming pools displayed signs that read "POSITIVELY NO FILIPINOS ALLOWED!"

Still, if the Philippines was America's "first real temptation," as Mark Twain wrote, then America, given its imperialist history, also became a temptation for Filipinos eager to escape poverty and provide for their families. After all, if Americans could come and claim the Philippines, why can't Filipinos move to America?

Colorism cuts deep in any colonized country, and I was born to parents who were considered the *mestizos* (light-skinned ones) in their own families. I am the only child of Emelie Salinas and Jose Lito Vargas. Shortly after they got married, it became apparent that they had been too young to wed, much less have a child. From the start, their marriage was subsidized by their parents. My father was one of nine children; his mother, Dolores, was the second wife of Ramon, a businessman in the capital city of Manila. I don't remember ever meeting Ramon. My mother was the only daughter of Teofilo and Leonila, a lower-middle-class couple in Iba, a rural *barangay* (town) in Zambales, an agricultural province dotted with unlimited rice farms and the sweetest heart-shaped mangoes you'll ever taste. To this day, when I see mangoes at grocery stores I am reminded of Iba. All over Zambales were beautiful rivers with crystalline waters where we bathed and washed our laundry. Teofilo was a high school dropout; Leonila did not make it past sixth grade. My parents separated before I learned to speak, and, if family lore is to be believed, the first words I ever spoke were "Lolo" and "Lola." As the first *apo* (grandchild) of Teofilo and Leonila, I was treasured, treated as if I were their own child.

If you lived in Zambales at the time, there were three primary ways to get to America: (1) join the U.S. Navy; (2) marry a U.S. citizen; (3) get petitioned by a relative. Lolo's younger sister, Florie, fell in love with an American who served in the U.S. Marines. They married, and Florie headed to America in 1963, becoming a U.S. citizen by 1966. When Florie asked Lolo if he wanted to come to America and bring his family, Lolo did not hesitate. Across the developing country, which was mired in political corruption, people believed that going to America was the golden ticket to better jobs, better wages, a better life. Because of the 1965 Immigration and Nationality Act, which ended decades-long racial and ethnic quotas and favored family unification, Florie was able to file a petition to bring Lolo to the United States. The wait took more than a decade. In 1984, when I was three years old, Lolo and Lola left Zambales for California.

The only things I've ever gotten from my father were his name and his thick eyebrows. By the time Lolo and Lola left, Papa had abandoned Mama and me. For as long as I can remember, Mama and his parents cared for me. Since she was the daughter in the family, who was expected to marry and have kids, Lolo told Mama to drop out of school so her younger brother could go to college. (Lolo could only afford to send one kid to school.) Mama left me in the care of relatives as she looked for odd jobs, which were hard to find for a woman with no college degree. After a while, Lolo and Lola told Mama to stop trying to find work and focus on raising me. They began supporting us. The Philippines is one of the world's largest recipients of remittances; Lolo and Lola were among the estimated 3.5 million Filipinos in the U.S. who would send monthly remittances that the Philippine economy could not survive without, creating a culture of consumerism and a cycle of financial dependency that I was part of before I even knew who I was.

As a toddler in Iba, before Lolo and Lola emigrated to America, I grew up in a house made of cement and wood with a makeshift bathroom. Running water was precious in the provinces, and we cleaned ourselves, including bathing, using the *tabo* system. *Tabo* are vessels used to take water from a *timba* (pail). That way, water is not wasted. (Before the Americans took over, coconut shells served as *tabo*. Americans introduced Filipinos to plastic, and plastic *tabo* were born.) Once Lolo and Lola moved to the U.S., Mama and I moved to Pasig, in the capital city, living in a rented apartment with running water—paid for, of course, by Lolo and Lola.

Growing up in Pasig, I thought of Lolo and Lola as wealthy people who had unlimited American dollars and an endless supply of M&M's candy and cans and cans of Spam, which they regularly shipped to us in a *balikbayan* (repatriate) box. It was not until I arrived in California to live with them that I discovered that they were not rich. In fact, they barely survived, working low-paying jobs: she as a food server, he as a security guard. To this day, I don't know how they managed to stretch every earned dollar. They didn't own a sprawling home, as I had imagined, but rented a modest three-bedroom house from Lolo's sister Florie. One of the bedrooms was for Lolo and Lola; one bedroom I shared with Uncle Rolan, my mother's younger brother; and the third bedroom they rented out to a friend. Lolo usually worked the overnight shift, while Lola and Uncle Rolan worked during the day. After school, I was in charge of raking the leaves from the lawn, taking out the trash, and making sure the dishes were always washed. If I'd been an obedient son in Pasig, I was an even more obedient grandson in Mountain View. In my mind, it was all I could do to support Lolo and Lola as they struggled to make ends meet, paying all their monthly bills while continuing to support Mama with a monthly allowance. Uncle Rolan, who worked in accounting, paid for whatever expenses I needed at school. At this point, Mama had a steady boyfriend named Jimmy, who worked overseas from time to time. Their daughter, Czarina, my half sister, was barely two years old when I left. Two years after I came to America, they had a son, Carl, my half brother, whom I have yet to meet in person. Jimmy helped raise them and continues to provide support.

Even though Lolo and Lola arrived in the U.S. nearly a decade before I did, I was their introduction to America—which is typical in intergenerational immigrant families trying to find their footing in their adopted home. Our home was decidedly Filipino. Lola could tell you the news from Manila, but would struggle to explain what was happening in San Francisco, just an hour north of us. We spoke either Tagalog or Sambali, the dialects spoken by the people of Zambales. We ate only Filipino food, mostly rice, fish, and pork. We mostly interacted with Filipino friends and relatives. We used the *tabo* system even though we had running water.

Google was founded less than two miles from our house, which is not too far from Stanford University. Mountain View is near the geographic heart of Silicon Valley, the storied region in the San Francisco Bay Area that runs on engineers and entrepreneurs placing their bets as they search for the next new thing. I grew up in the poorer part of Mountain View in the 1990s, before Apple, in nearby Cupertino, was dubbed "the most valuable brand in the world," and before Facebook, in nearby Menlo Park, would revolutionize the social media era. These days, renting an apartment can cost upward of three thousand dollars a month, and you'd be hard-pressed to buy a home for less than a million dollars. On any given day, at any given time, you'll spot a few Teslas on the road.

But my family is from the *other* Mountain View, which is part of the *other* Silicon Valley. This is the Mountain View of immigrant families who live in cramped houses and apartments, who depend on Univision, Saigon TV News, and the Filipino Channel for news of home, not the homes they're living in but the homes they left behind. This is the Silicon Valley of ethnic grocery stores in nondescript and dilapidated buildings, where sacks of rice and pounds of pork are cheaper, where you hear some Spanish, Tagalog, and Vietnamese before you hear a word of English. This is the *other* Mountain

View, in the *other* Silicon Valley, where the American Dream rests on the outdated and byzantine immigration system that requires families to wait for years, if not decades, to be reunited with their loved ones.

Where I grew up, Filipinos who populated public schools struggled to figure out where we belonged in an America that sees itself as mostly black and white. If America is a wobbly three-legged stool, with white Americans and black Americans each taking a leg, the third leg is divided between Latinos and Asians, whose histories of struggle and oppression are often maligned and neglected. I'm not sure which leg Native Americans would stand on. As for the Filipinos, we are stuck in the middle of one leg of that wobbly stool.

6.
Mexican José and Filipino Jose

"Where's your green card?" Mexican José was asking me.

We were sitting in the very back of the room. It was seventh-period science class, and Mr. Album was doing his best to keep everyone awake.

"Huh?" I snapped back, totally confused. "What?"

In my classes at Crittenden, there were only two Joses: Mexican José and Filipino Jose. Me.

"Your green card," Mexican José said, before pulling a plastic-covered card from his back pocket. "It's the card you need to bring with you to school. You know, if you're an immigrant."

I remembered the short television ads I'd been seeing at home, playing over and over again. The ads were about Proposition 187, a ballot initiative that sought to ban "illegal" people from using public services. The 1994 race for California governor was engulfed by Proposition 187. The Republican incumbent, Pete Wilson, was arguing that it was unfair for Americans to support "illegal immigrant children" attending American schools, costing taxpayers $1.5 billion a year. I remembered being confused by the ad. I didn't know who "illegal immigrant children" were and couldn't conceive of what $1.5 billion represented. Wilson said that his opponent, a Democrat named Kathleen Brown, would rather spend money on "illegals" than take care of "California's children." The ad ended by asking: "Where do you stand?"

Whenever "illegals" were brought up in the news, either on television or in the newspapers and magazines I scoured at the library, the focus was on Latinos and Hispanics, specifically Mexicans. It wasn't about Lolo and Lola, or Uncle Rolan and Uncle Conrad, or Lolo's younger sisters, Florie and Rosie. It wasn't about me. I didn't know that the immigration law that allowed my Filipino family to legally come here is the very same law that created "illegal immigration" as we know it. While the 1965 Immigration and Nationality Act benefited Asian immigrants, it put Latinos at a disadvantage. Before 1965, immigration from Mexico and other Latin American countries was largely unrestricted, and there was a government guest worker system called the bracero program that permitted millions of Mexican nationals to work in the U.S. The dissolution of the bracero program and the enactment of the 1965 immigration law created an "illegal immigrant" problem where there had been none.

I knew none of this as Mexican José showed me his green card.

All I knew was, I was not Mexican.

"I guess you don't have to worry about your green card," Mexican José told me a couple of minutes later. "Your name is Jose, but you look Asian."

7.

Fake

The next time I thought about my green card, I was riding my mountain bike to the nearby Department of Motor Vehicles office, just across the street from Target.

Without telling anyone in the family, I decided I was going to apply for a driver's permit. I was sixteen, the age when American teenagers were supposed to get their licenses. Sometimes, Lolo drove me to school but couldn't pick me up, so I often took the bus or bummed rides from friends. After Lolo bought me a newly painted black bike at a garage sale for fifty dollars, it was my primary way of getting around.

According to a DMV instruction booklet I had found at the library, I had to bring proof of identification with me. Since I was an immigrant, that meant bringing my green card, which Lolo kept in a folder in a filing cabinet in his bedroom. With my green card and a school identification card tucked inside my geometry textbook, I filled out the application form, took my seat, and waited for my name to be called.

A few minutes later, I handed a curly-haired, bespectacled woman my school ID and green card. Without even looking at the school ID—"Jose Vargas, Class of 2000, Mountain

View High School," it read—she examined the green card, flipping it around, twice. Furrowing her brows, she then lowered her head, leaned over, and whispered, "This is fake. Don't come back here again."

Fake.

Instantly, I thought she was mistaken, perhaps even lying. She seemed surprised that I didn't know that the green card was fake. In fact, I was so sure that she was mistaken or lying that I didn't even bother to question her. I just assumed she was wrong, turned around, got on my bike, and pedaled home, accompanied by a mixtape of Alanis Morissette and Boyz II Men, the music and lyrics muddling my thoughts.

Of course she's lying.

How can it be fake?

As I approached Mi Pueblo, a Mexican market where Lola and I sometimes shopped for mangoes and rice, my heart stopped.

Maybe the woman at the DMV thought I was Mexican? Because, you know, my name is Jose even though it's not José?

I returned home, my confusion starting to turn into a full-fledged panic attack. But I was sure everything would be fine. Lolo would clear everything up as he always did. Lolo had always taken care of everyone in the family. He stood no more than five feet seven inches tall but loomed over everyone, speaking in a clipped, overenunciated English that exuded clarity. Since Lolo worked the graveyard shift, he was often home in the afternoon. He was hunched over a table in the garage, cutting grocery coupons from newspapers, a cigarette dangling from his lips, when I arrived. I dropped my bike on the ground, searched for the green card in my backpack, and ran toward him.

"Peke ba ito?" I asked in Tagalog. ("Is this fake?") I held out the green card and searched his face as my voice cracked, afraid of what he might say.

Without addressing the question, he got up, swiped the card from my hand, and uttered a sentence that changed the course of my life.

"Huwag mong ipakita yang sa mga tao." ("Don't show it [the card] to people.")

His voice was soft, soaking in shame.

"Hindi ka dapat nandito." ("You are not supposed to be here.")

More than two decades later, remembering the shock of hearing that sentence, spoken by the very man who had sacrificed so much to bring his first grandson to America, still haunts me. Nothing Lolo ever said to me afterward—nothing Lola or Mama has said to me since—weighed as heavily.

I was speechless. In English and Tagalog. I don't remember what I said. But so many questions came darting from all directions that I thought my head would burst open to make room for them.

If this green card is "fake," then what else is "fake"?

Who else knows that this card is "fake"? Lola? Uncle Rolan? Does Mama know? Why didn't anybody tell me?

Can I get a "real" green card?

Is a "real" green card something you can buy?

For how much?

Where?

Can I tell my friends about this?

Can I trust my family?

Who can I trust?

All I knew was that I could barely trust myself—what I was feeling and how I was dealing with the shock. It was disorienting, as though gravity had changed and I could float away. Nothing was as it seemed. No one was who I thought they were, least of all myself. I was confused. I was angry. Angry at myself for having gone to the DMV to begin with. Angry at Lolo for putting me in this position, a twisted Faustian bargain that was not of my making. Angry at Mama. They conspired to send me to America to give me a better life without realizing they had created a nightmare scenario for me.

And I was scared.

Above all, it was the hardening—the emotional hardening—that I remembered most from that afternoon and the subsequent days and weeks.

Something within me hardened, and it became a place no one else could go. That I would not allow anyone else to breach. I felt betrayed in ways I couldn't yet articulate to myself or fully face.

My first instinct was to run. But there was nowhere to go, no one else to stay with. Another idea I had was to fly back to the Philippines, to go home to Mama. But Lolo told me that even the passport I used to get to America was fake. The photo in that passport was mine, but the name was not. He then told me that he'd bought me another passport with my name on it but not my *complete* name. Instead of Jose Antonio Salinas Vargas, he put my name as Jose Antonio Abaga Vargas. Salinas was Lolo's last name, the middle name that I have on my birth certificate. Abaga was Lola's maiden name. In case we got caught in a lie, he did not want his name, the Salinas name, involved. Salinas is the maiden name of Florie, his beloved sister, and the reason Lolo and Lola were able to emigrate in the first place. Salinas is the last name of Conrad, his favorite nephew. Neither Lola Florie nor Uncle Conrad knew of Lolo's scheme. Together, the fake green card and the passports cost Lolo forty-five hundred dollars, a huge sum for a security guard who made five dollars an hour.

It took me time to make sense of the gravity of the deception, the layers of lies. I couldn't stay legally. I couldn't leave legally, either. I was trapped. A legal no-boy's-land.

Later that night, on a phone call with Mama, I demanded answers to questions I had never imagined I would have to ask. I found out that the "uncle" who accompanied me on the flight to America was a smuggler whom Lolo had paid. The morning I left the Philippines was so rushed because she hadn't known when I would be leaving. The smuggler didn't give an exact date or time. The plan was that the smuggler would call hours before my flight was set to depart. I had to be ready at all times. Unbeknownst to me, my suitcase had been packed for months.

They had to lie about me because they lied about everything else.

After Lolo arrived in America, he petitioned for his two children to follow: Mama and Uncle Rolan. But instead of listing Mama as a married woman, which she still was, at least in the eyes of the law, Lolo lied and listed her as single. As a legal resident, which he was at the time, he could not petition for his married children. Even more important, Lolo didn't care for my father, who had abandoned Mama and me; he didn't want my father to come here. Lolo lied on the petition.

The lie scared Lolo. He grew nervous that immigration officials would discover that Mama was married, jeopardizing not only her chances of coming here but also that of Uncle Rolan. Lolo withdrew Mama's petition. After Uncle Rolan legally came to America in 1991, Lolo tried to get my mother here through a tourist visa. But her application was denied three times. Mama was unemployed; she couldn't prove that she wouldn't just overstay her visa and illegally stay in America, because she had nothing substantial to come back to. So, at Lolo's urging, she decided to send me to America with a smuggler. She figured she would find some way to follow me soon, within months, maybe a year at most, as she had promised that morning at the airport. But she couldn't find a way.

Their plan was to buy time until I could become legal. Lolo expected me to work under-the-table jobs. Maybe at the flea market where his older brother, David, and his wife, Modesta—Uncle Conrad's parents—cleaned bathrooms. *"Maganda ang trabaho iyan,"* Lolo said. ("It's a decent job.") Or maybe as a cashier at Fry's Electronics, where one of his friends was a supervisor. Once I had a job, Lola said I would find a woman who was a U.S. citizen to marry. That was the way to "get legal" and become a "citizen." I would save up money to pay the woman. Maybe I wouldn't even need to pay her, because I might even fall in love with her.

"Hindi ko gagawin niyan," I told Mama on the phone. ("I'm not doing it.")

"Hindi ako magpapakasal." (I'm not getting married.")

Shortly after that unforgettable day, I would learn that in Filipino culture, there's a term for someone who is in America illegally: "TNT," short for *tago ng tago*, which translates to "hiding and hiding." Finding out I was a TNT was not only the beginning of the lies I had to tell and what I had to do to "pass" as "American," but the beginning of the way I hid myself from Lolo, Lola, and Mama.

8.
Coming Out

One lie was enough. One lie was already too much. What I couldn't tell my family was that I did not want to marry a woman to "get legal" and become a "citizen" because I am gay.

"Sino ang kinakausap mo sa telepono?" Lola asked me as I headed to the bathroom late one night after I had found about the fake papers and all the lies it had taken to get me here. ("Who were you talking to on the phone?")

Now it was my turn to lie.

"It's just a friend from school," I answered in English. At that point, I had stopped replying in Tagalog to Lolo and Lola. It was one way to exert control. Independence.

"Bakit ganoon ka magsalita?" Lola asked. ("Why were you talking like that?")

"Like what?"

I was about to open the bathroom door when Lola grabbed my right hand to stop me. Her eyes started tearing up as she said: *"Apo ko, ayokong pumunta ka sa impiyerno."* ("Grandson, I don't want you to go to hell.")

I said nothing. I proceeded to go inside the bathroom. I stayed there until Lola went back to her room.

Like many gay teenagers of the late 1990s, I discovered I was gay because of Men4Men chat rooms on America Online (AOL). Usually around 11 P.M., when everyone in the house was already asleep, I chatted with all types of men: openly gay men, straight but curious men, still-in-the-closet men, married men, men of all ages. A few of the chats led to late-night phone calls.

I lied about my name and age when I messaged with guys directly, just one-on-one. I told guys that my name was Joey and that I was twenty-one years old. Young and much better-looking guys weren't interested in chatting with me once I described what I looked like, which I didn't lie about. I was chubby, which I've been since I was a kid. So the only guys who really wanted to chat with me online and possibly meet me in person were older guys, in their thirties and forties, most of them married and still in the closet. I didn't want to scare them by saying that I was sixteen.

There are many parts that make each of us whole. Since I didn't know who to talk to, or what to do, or how to think about the "illegal" part of me, embracing the gay part kept me alive. If I had not accepted it as early as I did, I don't know where I would be. Part of the self-acceptance came from what I was reading, watching, and consuming. I'll never forget seeing the bright and smiling face of a white woman on the cover of *Time* magazine as I was standing at Walgreens, not too far from our house. It was April 1997. The cover hit me like a freight truck. The headline—"Yep, I'm Gay"—could have been a lighthouse. The woman's name was Ellen DeGeneres.

Seeing Ellen on that *Time* cover had a profound impact on me. She provided a real name, a human face, a specific story. I bought the magazine and stuffed it in my backpack between my algebra and chemistry books, afraid someone at school would see it and figure me out.

But the sentimental high of Ellen's coming-out story was followed by the tragic low of Matthew Shepard's murder.

Shepard, a student at the University of Wyoming, was beaten, his pistol-whipped body tied to a fence, where he was left to die. This was in October 1998. Shepard's murder drew international headlines, even catching Lola's attention. When Lola asked me if I'd heard about the student who was killed for being *bakla* (gay), I nodded and walked away.

There's nothing wrong with being gay.

I don't know how exactly many times I must have said it to myself, like some kind of personal anthem, in the subsequent months. *There's nothing wrong with being gay.* I said it enough times to myself that, on May 27, 1999, I ended up blurting it out loud as I sat in the back of room 102 during U.S. history class.

Mr. Farrell had just shown the class a documentary on Harvey Milk, the first openly gay San Francisco city council member, who was shot and killed in 1978. He was just beginning the class discussion when I raised my hand and told my classmates, "I am gay."

Some of my classmates turned around. A student named Anna started to cry. She told the class about her gay uncle. Even though I felt how uncomfortable some people were, I remember feeling quite comfortable, as if I had opened a window and let some light into what was a very dark room—the room inside my head.

With that announcement, I became the only openly gay student at Mountain View High School. The declaration caused even more tension with Lola and especially with Lolo. As Catholics, they viewed homosexuality as a sin. Lolo said he was embarrassed about having *ang apo na bakla* ("a grandson who is gay"). Equally upsetting to Lolo was that I was making matters more difficult for myself, he said. He reiterated his plan: marry a woman, a U.S. citizen, and "get legal."

"I'm not doing that," I said to him as I sat in the passenger seat of his Toyota Camry. Minutes went by and the air got tighter and thicker. We stayed silent until he pulled over in front of the garage.

The engine was still running, and Lolo, with both hands on the steering wheel, said: *"Bahay ko ito."* ("This is my house.")

"Hindi pwede ang bakla sa bahay ko." ("Being gay is not allowed in my house.")

"You don't own me," I said.

He stopped the engine. Before he opened the door, he said: *"Wala kang utang na loob. Umalis ka dito."* ("You have no sense of gratitude. Get out of here.")

With only my backpack and less than twenty dollars in my wallet, I took off. I walked to the nearest Safeway and found a pay phone. I called "Peter," one of the older guys I'd met on AOL. We had started chatting for a few weeks before we met in person, at a coffee shop in downtown Mountain View. I asked Peter if I could crash at his place. When he said yes, I took two buses to get to his bungalow in Willow Glen, an upscale neighborhood in San Jose.

Peter was <u>thirty-eight</u>. He had been married for a few years before deciding to get a divorce, realizing that he needed to come out. We had an arrangement. I needed a place to stay for a couple of weeks, and he needed a companion.

Some people say that he took advantage of me.

I would argue that I took advantage of him.

PART II

Passing

1.
Playing a Role

I swallowed American culture before I learned how to chew it.

Being an American felt like a role I had to play, in an extemporaneous one-man play I made up after I found out I was not supposed to be in America.

Talk like an American.

Write like an American.

Think like an American.

Pass as an American.

I was the sixteen-year-old actor, producer, and director of this production, inhabiting a character that I honed with the help of a fourteen-inch TV set, a VCR, an audio player that played cassettes and CDs, and library cards from both the Mountain View Public Library and the Los Altos Library. Though there were libraries in the Philippines, I don't recall going into one while I was growing up. Here in America, the libraries were my church, and I was an acolyte. Between the two libraries—one with an extensive collection of videos of American films, the other boasting every CD you'd ever want to listen to—my education was complete. Lolo bought the secondhand TV set at a garage sale for thirty-five dollars. As a birthday gift, Lolo and Lola bought me the brand-new VCR that could record TV shows.

What I watched on TV led to what movies I looked for, what music I listened to, what books, magazines, and newspapers I read. The first source of confusion was magazines, which were prominently displayed at both libraries. I was confused about the difference between *Time, Newsweek, The New Yorker, The New Republic, The Atlantic,* and *Commentary,* in the same way that I couldn't figure out what distinguished the TV channels from one another. Deepening the confusion was trying to understand the Israeli-Palestinian conflict, which dominated the headlines at the time. I struggled to understand what was going on. There is no such thing as winter in the Philippines—no ice, no snow—so I was instantly drawn to figure skating. I couldn't believe people were spinning and jumping on a quarter-inch of a blade. The saga of Nancy Kerrigan and Tonya Harding made competitive skating more popular; there was always a competition every weekend. Before skaters began their "programs," the titles of the music they skated to were flashed on TV. Skating was my introduction to Rachmaninoff, Beethoven, Mozart, et al. Did you know there are two versions of *Romeo and Juliet,* the Tchaikovsky version and the Prokofiev version? I borrowed all of it from the library. It was free. I couldn't believe it was free. Listening to rap and hip-hop while trying to understand Alanis Morissette and Joni Mitchell was my passport to black *and* white America; I thought that if I was fluent in both cultures, speaking in both tongues, no one would ask where I was from and how I got here. (It took me a while to discover that Alanis and Joni were both Canadians.) The 1990s was the beginning

MUSIC, Magazines, Many

of hip-hop's rise as the most popular genre of music, particularly among young people. I convinced myself that reciting the lyrics to every one of Lauryn Hill's and Tupac Shakur's songs was proof of my American-ness. When I heard about a thing called country music, and couldn't find that much country music at the libraries, I went to Tower Records and listened to songs by Garth Brooks and Dolly Parton.

For me, movies were like a field trip, a way of seeing just how vast the country is. In a span of a few weeks, I watched *Goodfellas, Hannah and Her Sisters, Do the Right Thing,* and *Working Girl.* I was floored when I realized that they were all filmed in a place called New York City. How can Martin Scorsese's New York City be the same as Woody Allen's New York City, which is not the same thing as Spike Lee's New York City and Mike Nichols's New York City? That was my introduction to perspective. After watching *Sophie's Choice, Silkwood, Out of Africa,* and *A Cry in the Dark,* I went up to a librarian and asked: "Is there more than one Meryl Streep?"

Watching TV was a different kind of cultural immersion. *TV Guide,* a weekly magazine that I bought at the grocery store, was a bible. TV is where I picked up idioms and mannerisms. I learned how to use "cool beans" from *Full House.* In order to act, talk, and pass as some kind of American, I studied every show I could watch, from *Frasier* to *Roseanne,* from *The Fresh Prince of Bel-Air* to *The West Wing.* Appropriating how Charlie Rose and Bill Moyers spoke on PBS while listening to Tupac and Lauryn in my CD player seemed as far away from the "illegal" Filipino with a thick accent as I could get.

Airing back-to-back on weekday afternoons, *The Rosie O'Donnell Show* and *The Oprah Winfrey Show* unlocked doors in my imagination. Oprah's show introduced me to authors like Maya Angelou, Wally Lamb, and Toni Morrison—oh, how Oprah loved Morrison, whose books she often selected for her book club. I was drawn to Angelou because she bore a resemblance to Lola, with the same low and rich timbre of a voice. Almost daily, Rosie's show featured someone from Broadway, including the actress and singer Audra McDonald, whose voice was so expansive—swinging and soaring, walloping and wailing—it seemed to jump out of the screen and into my bedroom.

I didn't know what Broadway was, or how the Tony Awards differed from the Oscars or the Emmys, but because of McDonald, I recorded the 1998 Tony Awards on TV, which Rosie hosted. About twenty minutes into the show, just as I was figuring out the difference between "Best Revival of a Play" and "Best New Play," O'Donnell introduced a musical called *Ragtime*.

Over a simple melody, a young boy took center stage, later to be joined by his father and mother and other white people from a place called New Rochelle, New York. Together, they sang:

The skies were blue and hazy.
Rarely a storm.
Barely a chill.
The afternoons were lazy.
Everyone warm. Everything still.
The days were gently tinted,
Lavender pink, lemon and lime.
Ladies with parasols.

Fellows with tennis balls.
There were gazebos.
And there were no Negroes.

A beat later, the music changed to a syncopated tune, and a group of black people danced center stage and sang: *"And everything was Ragtime! Listen to the Ragtime!"*

Then a black man sitting in front of a piano took over. He declared: *"Up in Harlem, people danced to a music that was theirs and no one else's. The sound of changing time. The music of a better day."*

Then the white people, on the other side of the stage, took over the melody and sang:

Ladies with parasols,
Fellows with tennis balls.
There were no Negroes
And there were no immigrants.

Yet again the music changed, signaling the arrival of something mysterious as a new group of people—immigrants—took center stage. A bearded man with some kind of accent (I couldn't place where it was from) said:

They came from Western and Eastern Europe by the
*   thousands.*
No dream was too big.
They would be the next J. P. Morgan, Evelyn Nesbit or
*   Henry Ford. It would be their century, too. It was*
*   only 1906.*

My mind raced as the white people, the black people, and the immigrants crowded the stage and all together sang:

And there were ninety-four years to go!
And there was music playing,
Catching a nation in its prime.
Beggar and millionaire,
Everyone, everywhere
Moving to the Ragtime!

At this point, members of the three groups started spreading out, then began to self-segregate, before finally moving into separate areas of the stage while the music's melody turned dissonant and discordant. With white people back at center stage, as black people took stage left while immigrants took stage right, they all sang:

And there was distant music
Skipping a beat, singing a dream.
A strange, insistent music
Putting out heat,
Picking up steam.
The sound of distant thunder
Suddenly starting to climb . . .
It was the music
Of something beginning,
An era exploding,
A century spinning
In riches and rags,
And in rhythm and rhyme.

The people called it Ragtime . . .
Ragtime!
Ragtime!
Ragtime!

I watched this performance so many times that I wore out the tape. The "immigrants" in the performance didn't look like Mexicans or Filipinos or Chinese or Indians or Pakistanis—what people usually think of when they hear "immigrants." It wasn't until watching that performance that I realized that white people were immigrants, too, that they came from somewhere: Ireland, Germany, Italy, Latvia, Russia, etc. Obsessing over *Ragtime* led to discovering the works of Oscar Hammerstein, Richard Rodgers, Irving Berlin, George Gershwin, and Stephen Sondheim, all of whom, I would realize, came from immigrant backgrounds. *Ragtime* connected dots I didn't know existed, allowing me to better understand American history in ways my textbooks didn't fully explain. I would learn that except for Native Americans, whose tribes were already here before the colonists and the Pilgrims landed, and African Americans, who were uprooted from their homes and imported to this country as slaves, everyone was an immigrant. I didn't know what legal papers they had, or if they needed them, or if they were considered "illegals," too, but white people were immigrants, like my family are immigrants. After doing some research at the libraries, I discovered that *Ragtime* was based on an historical novel by E. L. Doctorow, whose book told the changing story of America through real-life personalities and fictionalized characters at the turn of the twentieth century. Each time I watched the tape, every time I listened to the song, I wondered where Latinos, Asians, Africans, Caribbeans, Middle Easterners—the new immigrants of the past few decades—fit on that stage and in the evolving American story. I wondered where my Mexican friends fit. I wondered where Lolo, Lola, and I fit, if we fit at all.

We spoke Taglish at home—a combination of the Tagalog that Lolo and Lola spoke, and the answers I gave in English. Except for the 11 P.M. local news, Lolo and Lola watched only the Filipino Channel, a cable network that re-aired shows from the Philippines. Sometimes, I watched the shows with everyone. More often than not, though, I was in my room.

The only time I saw a Hollywood movie starring people who looked anything like my family was *The Joy Luck Club*, which, I learned later on, was based on a book by a Chinese American writer, Amy Tan. I picked up the movie at the video store, drawn by the VHS cover: the smiling faces of four Asian women and a striking shot of the Golden Gate Bridge. I rented the tape and watched it late one night in the living room when everyone was sleeping. After about a month of living with Peter, I returned to Lolo and Lola's house. We made peace, uneasy as it was. But the silence was too heavy, polluting the already suffocating air in the house.

We shared one bathroom. After Lola used the bathroom that night, she saw me in the living room. She sat down in the opposite side of the couch. We said nothing to each other. *The Joy Luck Club* was the first American film Lola and I watched together. I'm not sure how much she understood the interlocking stories of four Chinese women who emigrated to America in search of better lives. But she understood it enough that she started to cry when one of the characters, Lindo, broke into tears as she explained her love for her American-born daughter, Waverly. I ended up watching Lola watch the movie, wondering how much she had given up to come here, how rarely she got to see her own daughter. At that moment, I realized it wasn't just me who missed my mother—Lola longed for my mama, too. But I was too selfish to want to see it, too absorbed with my own pain.

In those early years, passing as American meant rejecting anything Filipino, at least outwardly. Lolo scoffed when he asked me a question in Tagalog, *"Saan ka pupunta?"* ("Where are you going?"), and I responded in English, "I'm going to the library."

Passing as an American was my way of exerting control over a life I had no control over. It was not my decision to come here, acquire fake papers, and lie my way into being in America. But I was here. At the very least, I felt that I had to control what kind of American I was going to be, what kind of cultural connections I was going to make, which led to what kind of mask I had to wear.

2.

Mountain View High School

The moment I realized that writing for newspapers meant having a "byline"—"by Jose Antonio Vargas," my name in print, on a piece of paper, visible and tangible—I was hooked.

There are no writers in my family—not on my mother's side, not on my father's side. In the Philippines, we're a family of farmers, nurses, cooks, accountants, construction workers, U.S. Navy veterans. I got into journalism because of a high school teacher.

"You ask too many annoying questions," Mrs. Dewar told me.

A self-described hippie with a smoky voice, Mrs. Dewar taught English composition to high school sophomores like me. Mrs. Dewar was also the longtime adviser to the *Oracle*, the student newspaper. A forty-something educator who'd had early aspirations of being a journalist, she informed me of a free, two-week journalism camp for "minority" journalists at San Francisco State University, her alma mater. When I asked her what a journalist does, she quipped, "It's for annoying people like you who love to ask questions."

First, it was a sign of rebellion and independence from my

family, a way of rejecting Lolo's strategy of working under-the-table jobs until I marry a woman and get my papers.

Second, and more importantly, writing was a form of existing, existing through the people I interviewed and the words I wrote as I struggled with where my physical being was supposed to be. Writing was also a way of belonging, a way of contributing to society while doing a public-service-oriented job that's the antithesis of the stereotype that "illegals" are here to take, take, take. I didn't realize it then, but the more stories I reported on, the more people I interviewed, the more I realized that writing was the freest thing I could do, unencumbered by borders and legal documents and largely dependent on my skills and talent. Reporting, interviewing, and writing felt like the safest, surest place in my everyday reality. If I was not considered an American because I didn't have the right papers, then practicing journalism—writing in English, interviewing Americans, making sense of the people and places around me—was my way of writing myself into America. In the beginning, writing was only a way of passing as an American. I never expected it to be an identity. Above all else, I write to exist, to make myself visible.

Instantly, journalism became not just a passion but *the* driving force in my life. Everything, and everyone, took a backseat to my work. Getting good grades at school took a backseat to my being a reporter. If it didn't have anything to do with furthering my career in journalism, I didn't do it. The myopia energized me, giving me the chutzpah (a word I first learned from Rosie's show) to advocate for myself. After returning from the "minority" summer camp of mostly Latino and black high school students, I cold-called the *Moun-*

tain View Voice, my local weekly community newspaper, and
talked my way into an unpaid internship. I was desperate to
get this internship. For a few weeks, all the job entailed was
answering the phones and buying coffee for the top editor, an
overworked man named Rufus Jeffris. But when a fire erupted
three blocks from where I lived and there were no other reporters to cover it, the editor sent me. My first-ever front-page
story was about a fire on Farley Street, where I grew up.

"Blackened scraps of clothing carefully piled on a corner
of the front lawn were the only items that Mitch and Linda
Radisich were able to salvage from their home at 1151 Farley
Street after a fire gutted the residence on June 16," read the
"lede" (the opening sentence) of the news story, which took
up a third of the entire front page. I was proud of that lede,
especially of the verbs "salvage" and "gutted." News writing,
especially breaking news writing, I learned early on, depended
on verbs. It was all about action.

"Anong ginagawa mo?" ("What are you doing?") Lolo ex-
claimed when he saw my byline on the front page of the *Voice.*

"Bakit nasa diyaryo ang pangalan mo?" ("Why is your
name in the newspaper?")

The angrier Lolo became, the more independent I felt. I
didn't need his approval. Even if I did, he couldn't give it. Lolo
had to ask me what "blackened" meant.

"Masyado ka nang nagiging sosyal," Lolo said. "You're getting fancy now."

Fancy or not, I made a concerted effort to stay as busy
as possible. The busier my schedule was, the more activities I
committed to, the less time I had to spend at home. Being at
home reminded me of my limitations. Being at school opened

up possibilities. In addition to writing for both the *Voice* and *Oracle*, I sang in choir, competed in speech and debate tournaments, acted and directed in plays and musicals, and was elected by the student government to represent their interests to the school board. I was so omnipresent at school that teachers, administrators, and parents of my classmates took notice. I neglected to tell Lolo and Lola about parent-teacher nights and open houses at school.

I went alone and represented myself. It was easier that way.

"Don't you ever go home?" Pat Hyland, the school principal, asked me one night after speech and debate practice. Because I was probably the busiest student at school who did not drive, classmates and school staff gave me rides, including Pat. Short-haired and quick-witted, Pat was the earliest member of a bighearted community of strangers who, over time, would occupy essential roles in my life. Whenever she drove me home, we stopped and got some lattes at Starbucks on El Camino Real Road.

El Camino Real is the artery that runs through the peninsula south of San Francisco, dividing communities by race and class and separating adequate schools from great ones. Residents on its east side were generally on the lower end of the economic ring, mostly service workers and laborers. Folks on the west side, particularly the western parts of Mountain View and its neighboring towns, Los Altos and Los Altos Hills, were considerably more affluent, white-collar professionals and technology entrepreneurs who cashed in early and felt comfortable buying their kids convertible BMWs and Mercedes-Benzes. The parents of well-to-do students were

generous to many students from working-class families like
mine, paying for field trips, no questions asked. To this day,
I don't know just how much Sandie and Art Whipple, whose
daughter, Ashley, I sang and acted with, spent to ensure that
I got to go on this and that trip. Fees for speech competitions
would be covered, with no trace of who paid for what. Karen
Keefer, my speech and debate coach, usually covered what I
couldn't pay for. For the most part, you couldn't find anyone to thank because they didn't need or want thanking. If
it sounds too benevolent to believe, just too good to be true,
perhaps it was. Nevertheless, I was a product of this community. Sometimes I wonder what would have happened to me if
I had not attended a relatively wealthy school in a community
of privilege.

Shortly after we met, Pat introduced me to Rich Fischer,
her boss, the school district's superintendent. Though he was
the highest-ranking official at the school, he wore his authority lightly. He was friendly and accessible, regularly roaming
the school grounds interacting with both students and teachers. "Don't call me Mr. Fischer," he said during our first meeting. "It's Rich." I was more comfortable with teachers and
administrators than I was with my classmates. Part of it was
because I was forced to grow up fast and had adult-size ambi-
tions that seemed bigger than getting good grades and getting
into a good college. I had to take care of myself. Another part
of it was because whenever I was with adults outside my family, I was the center of their attention. They engaged me in
ways that my grandparents did not and could not.

I was elected as the student representative on the school
board, which meant I ended up spending more time with

Rich. After he and his wife, Sheri, and their granddaughter, Alexis, attended a performance of *Lend Me a Tenor* in which I played a bellhop, they took an interest in me. Rich's longtime assistant, Mary Moore, scheduled biweekly lunches where we could catch up. The lunches led to dinners, and I got to know both Rich and Mary, whose relationship was less like boss and secretary than brother and sister. They were like a family unit, and they treated me like family. Over the years, Mary has written me more greeting cards—birthday cards, holiday cards, hope-you-feel-better cards—than anyone else I've ever met. Mary introduced me to her daughter, Daisy, and her son, C.J., both of whom are around my age. Because I was forced to grow up quickly, I befriended many adults, including Judy Hannemann and Susan Sweeley, who served on the school board.

"There is always one moment in childhood," Graham Greene once wrote, "when the door opens and lets the future in." As the years passed, Pat, Rich, Sheri, Alexis, Mary, Daisy, C.J., Susan, and Judy, among others, are the people who would find windows and try to open them when doors were shut. They did it because they could afford to; more importantly, they did it because they wanted to.

3.
An Adopted Family

"What do you mean you're not applying to college?" Pat asked. While on our regular Starbucks stop, she was wondering why I hadn't shared anything about my college plans. This was the end of junior year, the time of fretting over college admission tests, the time of planning college tours.

I told Pat that I was not planning to go to college. I said I had a job lined up after high school, covering city hall and writing feature stories for the *Voice*, which would pay me twenty-five and fifty dollars per article—a solid sum. I tried to sound proud of my plan, even though I felt defeated. College was never an option, especially after I found out that I was in the country illegally and that I couldn't apply for financial aid. But I couldn't tell Pat that. I had not told anyone except for Mrs. Denny, the choir teacher. Every spring the choir goes on tour. In the beginning of my junior year, Mrs. Denny announced to the class that we would be going to Japan. Shortly after, I pulled her to the corner of the room, near her desk, where no one could hear us.

"Mrs. Denny, I can't go to Japan."

"What do you mean?"

"I don't have the right papers."

"What are you talking about?"

She paused.

"We'll get you the right papers."

"No, no, you don't understand." I really didn't know what words to use, or if I could trust her with this information. All I could say was: "I don't have the right passport. I don't have the right green card."

Mrs. Denny's eyes parted like curtains. Her shoulders dropped. The only word she managed to say was, "Oh."

The following day, without giving me any warning, she told the whole class that the plan had changed. Instead of going to Japan, we would head to Hawaii. I don't remember if my classmates were disappointed or angry. What I will never get out of my mind was the reason that Mrs. Denny gave me when, years later, I asked her why she changed the plan: "I was not leaving any of my students behind."

All of the adults I knew at Mountain View High School wanted to make sure I wasn't left behind. Soon, everyone was asking about my college plans, including Gail Wade, the mother of one of my closest friends, Nathalie. Gail and I met while I was representing myself during a parent-teacher night, and our shared love for the Russian figure skater Maria Butyrskaya drew us closer, to the point that she started referring to herself as my "Jewish mom." Her house was only a few blocks from school, and Gail taught French at a nearby middle school. Sometimes, during our lunch breaks, she and I would meet at her house and watch tapes of skating competitions.

Without realizing it, I replaced Mama, to whom I barely

spoke at the time, with Pat, Sheri, Mary, and Gail. I couldn't talk to my own mother while I was collecting mother figures.

Eventually, I had to tell them the truth. I had no idea how they would react. I feared that they would reject me. One by one, I explained the fake green card, the fake passport, why I had to always bum rides to and from school, why college was not an option.

"Oh, now I understand why you don't drive," Rich said. "I couldn't figure out why."

This was in the early weeks of 2000, more than a year before legislation called the DREAM Act—short for the Development, Relief, and Education for Alien Minors Act, which would grant a path to legalization for children brought to the U.S. illegally—would be introduced in Congress. At this point, there were no Dreamers and no one called anyone "undocumented." Teachers and educators, especially in more affluent communities like Mountain View, did not have much experience with the issue, much less know what to do with someone like me.

Pat and Rich spoke to lawyers separately; their families considered adopting me. Mary and Gail considered adoption, too. But it was too late. Their lawyers said that because I was already over the age of sixteen, adoption wouldn't fix the problem. According to the lawyers, Lolo and Lola could have adopted me before I turned sixteen had they known it was an option. Although they were naturalized U.S. citizens, Lolo and Lola were wary of lawyers and fearful of the U.S. legal system. Mary's daughter, Daisy, offered to marry me even though she knew I was gay. I declined, lovingly.

At the time, I felt disconnected from Lolo and Lola and

didn't know how to process this information. I was too numb
to feel anger or heartbreak. I was so ashamed of myself, so
ashamed of Lolo and Lola—of the situation that was created
for me, a situation that I didn't know how to solve—that I
never bothered to introduce them to the family I discovered
at Mountain View High School. I was too young to realize
that the dream that Mama, Lolo, and Lola had for me was
dictated by their own realities, by their own sense of limitations. The America they dreamed for me was not the America
I was creating for myself.

If my adult mentors couldn't adopt me, they were deter-
mined to figure out a way to send me to college. They did,
identifying a scholarship program that did not ask or care
about my immigration status, established by a venture capital-
ist named Jim Strand, whose kids attended my school district.
I received a four-year scholarship to college. Soft-spoken and
taciturn, Jim met me at Peet's Coffee in downtown Los Altos.
He told me there were no criteria for the scholarship; he didn't
care whether or not I had the right papers. The only thing
that mattered was whether I really wanted to go to college and
needed help. "Thank you very much," I said, and insisted on
buying him the iced coffee. I had chosen to go to San Francisco State, which had hosted the summer camp that jump-
started my journalism career. But that wasn't the only reason
why. After finding out that my green card was fake—that the
Alien Registration Number was not mine—I never wanted
to be associated with a number. So unlike most, if not all,
of my college-bound classmates, I didn't take the SATs, the
college admissions test. As it happened, San Francisco State
didn't care about SAT scores so long as my grade point aver-

age was higher than 3.0. Since I already had a career, at least in my mind, I didn't really care much about grades or GPAs. Thankfully, mine ended up being higher than 3.0. It was 3.4.

As it turned out, I was the very first recipient of what is now called the MVLA Scholars. Jim donated $1 million over five years to seed the scholarship, and other parents and philanthropists have continued to fund it since. Since its inception eighteen years ago, more than 350 students have received support from the scholarship. According to the scholarship's administrators, all of whom are volunteers from the community, about 98 percent of the 137 students that they are currently supporting are the first in their family to attend college in America. Of those 137 students, 36 happen to be undocumented. Along with Jim, I now serve on the scholarship's advisory board.

4.

Breaking the Law

The first time I willfully broke the law, I was sitting in a small conference room on the third floor of the *San Francisco Chronicle* building.

It was spring 2000. I was just about to graduate from high school and was planning on moving to San Francisco for college. A journalist named Teresa Moore, who had edited articles I had submitted to a youth magazine, suggested I get an entry-level job at the *Chronicle*, where she had been a reporter. I'd answer the phone and deliver people's mail and faxes, but Teresa said I could also pitch freelance articles on the side. In was in. "There's nothing like working inside a big newsroom," she told me.

Before I allowed myself to say no—before I dared explain to Teresa that I didn't have the right legal documents to work—I found myself inside the *Chronicle* building filling out an employment form. Until that point, I had only been volunteering or doing contract jobs, nothing serious, certainly nothing that required legal paperwork. Since my discovery at the DMV, I avoided talking about paperwork, just as I avoided any conversation about driving. I had never filled out an employment form before.

The form asked for my full name, home address, date of birth, and phone number. That was the easy part.

Then came two dreaded statements, both in bold letters. The first:

☐ I am aware that federal law provides for imprisonment and/or fines for false statements or use of false documents in connectŠn with the completŠn of this form.

The second:

☐ I attest, under penalty of perjury, that I am (check one of the following boxes):

They were followed by boxes, one of which I was supposed to check:

☐ A citizen or natŠnal of the United States
☐ A lawful permanent resident (Alien #) A
☐ An alien authorized to work untÕ
  (Alien # or AdmissŠn #)

I am not a "lawful permanent resident." I am also not "an alien authorized to work." My "alien registration number," the number on the fake green card that Lolo bought me, belongs to someone else. I didn't know if that person is dead or alive; I didn't know what risk I would put that person in if I had used the number. I hated that I didn't know what I didn't know, and that I could potentially hurt someone. The only choice left was box number one, which was not really a choice because I am not a U.S. citizen. Not by birth. Not by law. Later, I would also learn that, under 18 USC § 911, it is "a criminal offense for anyone to falsely and willfully impersonate a citizen of the United States." Moreover, "whoever falsely and willfully represents himself to be a citizen of the United States shall be _fined_ under this title or _imprisoned_ not more than three years, or both."

But I wanted the job.

It meant _independence, from Lolo and Lola, from Mama._

I needed the job.

Sweating under my brow, a couple of drops staining the form, I checked box number one.

Naïve as it sounds, I remember thinking: _Yes, I am lying. But I am to going to earn this box._

I don't remember how many times I said it to myself: _I am going to earn this box._

What I always remember is hearing people say that people like me should "earn" our citizenship.

Exactly how I would earn being a citizen, I had no idea. What I did know, however, was that Lolo's lies were now my lies. I was no longer the blameless kid who wasn't aware of the circumstances of how I arrived in America. I was now a nineteen-year-old making a difficult and necessary choice to survive, which meant breaking the law.

What would you have done? Work under the table? Stay under the radar? Not work at all?

Which box would you check?

What have you done to earn your box?

Besides being born at a certain place in a certain time, did you have to do anything?

Anything at all?

If you wanted to have a career, if you wanted to have a life, if you wanted to exist as a human being, what would you have done?

5.

The Master Narrative

"The problem with living outside the law," Truman Capote once wrote, "is that you no longer have its protection."

I never felt protected by the law.

I didn't understand why the law was the way it was.

To pass as an American, I always had to question the law. Not just break it, not just circumvent it, but question it. I had to interrogate how laws are created, how illegality must be seen through the prism of who is defining what is legal for whom. I had to realize that throughout American history, legality has forever been a construct of power.

Lynchings, violent seizures of indigenous land, barring women from voting—all of that was legal. Until very recently, marriage between people of the same sex was not only considered immoral, it was illegal. "Separate but equal" was legal. Jim Crow was the law of the land.

In 1954, Border Patrol agents showed up unannounced at citrus farms, cattle ranches, and factories with the goal of deporting as many Mexicans as possible. The whole effort, called Operation Wetback, was legal.

The first peoples who populated this land, Native Americans, were not considered United States citizens until 1924, when the Indian Citizenship Act was passed.

The Chinese Exclusion Act of 1882, the first law implemented to prevent a specific ethnic group from immigrating to America, was not repealed until 1943.

The Naturalization Act of 1790, our country's first set of laws dealing with citizenship, said that an applicant had to be "a free white person" of "good moral character" to be a U.S. citizen.

Three years prior to that, in 1787, the U.S. Constitution required that escaped slaves be returned to their owners. Black slaves.

There it was again: "black" and "white."

I didn't realize it as such, but I was struggling to understand the construction of that binary, trying to unlock why "white" and "black" became an obsession for me, which was fueled even more when I first read Toni Morrison's *The Bluest Eye*.

I was assigned to read the book in eighth grade when I joined an after-school book club led by Mr. Zehner, who taught language arts and U.S. history. A core group of ten students attended, including Sabiha Basrai, the smartest girl in my class. Her parents, Rashida, a graphic designer, and Farukh, a filmmaker, both immigrants from India, often gave me rides after school. As it happened, the book club was Farukh's idea; he challenged Mr. Zehner to challenge his students to do more rigorous reading. We were assigned to read books—one book each month—that Mr. Zehner considered provocative and controversial while being comprehensible yet above our reading level. His list fit the criteria, from Hermann Hesse's *Siddhartha* to Erich Maria Remarque's *All Quiet on the Western Front* to Ken Kesey's *One Flew Over the Cuckoo's Nest*.

No book stimulated me more than Morrison's. *The Bluest Eye* was a puzzle: the way the book began, evoking the Dick-and-Jane-and-Mother-and-Father photograph from basic reading primers I knew nothing about; the way it was structured (the book was divided into four parts, each a season of the year); the way Morrison revealed the entire plot of the book on the very first page (Pecola Breedlove, the eleven-year-old at the center of the story, is impregnated by her own father, and she will live and her child will die); the way Morrison used language, including the italics that open the narrative. "There is really nothing more to say—except *why*," Morrison writes. "But since *why* is difficult to handle, one must take refuge in *how*."

The "how" of the story is Pecola being told that she is ugly, unattractive, unwanted. She takes it all in, so much that she wishes for blue eyes.

The "why" of the story haunted me. Why was Pecola wishing for blue eyes when she had black ones? Who told her to want blue eyes? Why did she believe them?

I would come back to Pecola's story again and again, unlocking whatever meaning I could find. In the pages of *The Bluest Eye,* Pecola was a year younger than I was when I came to the U.S. Our lives couldn't have been any more different, save for one central detail: we were both lied to.

Hers was the lie that blue eyes were better, that she was not enough.

I didn't recognize the lies that made up my life until a year after reading about Pecola. By that time, I had become aware of the fact that I didn't have legal documents to be in this country, that I was "illegal." The word was ubiquitous, always floating in the air. "Illegal" was what the news media called us, from the television and radio news programs I consumed to the newspapers I read at the school library to the magazines I would lose myself in at the public libraries. The word, I discovered, was more than an identification—it carried meaning, signifying what I could not do. Being "illegal" meant not being able to drive, like most of my classmates. Being "illegal" translated to limitations of what my life was and what it could be.

While watching PBS, I ran across a replay of an interview, held at the New York Public Library, between Morrison and the journalist Bill Moyers. The show was called *A World of Ideas*. I was so stunned by the exchange that I searched for the transcript.

Moyers: I don't think I've ever met a more pathetic creature in contemporary literature than Pecola Breedlove. . . . Abused by her—

Morrison: Everybody.

Moyers: —parents, rejected by her neighbors, ugly, homely, alone. Finally descending into madness. . . . It's been years since I read that novel, but I remember her.

Morrison: She surrendered completely to the so-called master narrative.

Moyers: To?

Morrison: The master narrative, I mean, the whole notion of what is ugliness, what is worthlessness, what is contempt. She got it from her family, she got it from school, she got it from the movies, she got it everywhere.

Moyers: The master narrative. What is—that's life?

Morrison: No, it's white male life. The master narrative is whatever ideological script that is being imposed by the people in authority on everybody else. The master fiction. History. It has a certain point of view. So, when these little girls see that the most prized gift that they can get at Christmastime is this little white doll, that's the master narrative speaking. *"This is beautiful, this is lovely, and you're not it."* . . . She is so needful, so completely needful, has so little, needs so much, she becomes the perfect victim.

At the age of nineteen, when I started lying about who I was so I could pass as an American, I did not have any authority. The only history I knew of was my own, which I was still struggling to make sense of. But after watching the interview and reading the transcript, I decided that I must not play "the perfect victim"—in my mind, "victim" and "illegal" were one and the same. I convinced myself that someone, somewhere, somehow created "the master narrative" of illegality: human beings identified as "illegals," as if one's existence can be deemed unlawful; "illegals" serving Americans, either by babysitting their kids, or trimming their lawns, or constructing their houses, or harvesting their crops—the images and visuals perpetuated by the news media, corroborated in TV

shows and movies; human beings being told what they cannot do and where they cannot go. Understanding the experience of black people in America—why black was created
so people could be white—pried open how Latinos, Asians,
Native Americans, and other marginalized groups have been
historically oppressed through laws and systems that had little
or nothing to do with what was right. White as the default,
white as the center, white as the norm, is the central part of
the master narrative. The centrality of whiteness—how it
constructed white versus black, legal versus illegal—hurts not
only people of color who aren't white but also white people
who can't carry the burden of what they've constructed.

The Bluest Eye, I would learn, was Morrison's first book.
Often, her books, from Sula to Song of Solomon to Beloved, were
not displayed alongside books by Ernest Hemingway, William Faulkner, F. Scott Fitzgerald, or writers who make up the
canon of American literature taught at schools. Too often, while
searching for her work, I was directed to the African American
sections of bookstores. Searching for Morrison led me to discover the work of black poets like Langston Hughes and Paul
Laurence Dunbar, to the writings of black writers like Ralph
Ellison, Alice Walker, and James Baldwin. I cite their race because it's a crucial element of their power. Black writers gave me
permission to question America. Black writers challenged me to
find my place here and created a space for me to claim. Reading
black writers opened doors to other writers of color, specifically
Asian and Latino authors (Carlos Bulosan, Sandra Cisneros,
Arundhati Roy, to name just a few) whose work was often even
more marginalized than that of black writers.

Indeed, if Morrison provoked me to ask more penetrat-

ing questions—to insist on the "how" and the "why"—
Baldwin challenged my very core. I read these words from
Baldwin like they were some sort of dare: "You have to de-
cide who you are, and force the world to deal with you, not
its idea of you."

I wanted no part of the master narrative about who the
"illegal" is.

I would take refuge in creating my own.

6.

Ambition

The more ambitious as a reporter I became, the more risks I had to take, the more lies I had to tell, the more laws I had to break.

A few months after landing the entry-level job at the *Chronicle,* I applied for a paid summer internship at the *Philadelphia Daily News* in 2001. When Debi Licklider, the recruiter, asked if I had a driver's license and if I could drive, I lied and said "yes" to both. While working in Philadelphia, covering the police beat and writing breaking news stories, I took cabs and rode buses and the subway to get to my assignments. A couple of times I had to hitchhike, making sure that no one found out. I couldn't tell the editors that I didn't have a license.

The 9/11 attacks changed immigration, legal and illegal, making it more difficult for people to come to America. In 2002, I applied and was accepted for another paid summer internship, this time at the *Seattle Times.* Patricia Foote, the recruiter, emailed the summer interns to remind us to bring our proof of citizenship on our first day at work: a birth certificate, a passport, or a driver's license, plus an original Social

Security card. I immediately called her. I took a leap of faith
and told her about my immigration status. She sounded surprised and perplexed. And sympathetic—at least she sounded
like it on the phone. She told me she had to consult a lawyer
at the office and would get back to me. When she called, she
rescinded the offer.

I didn't know this woman. Effectively, she was a
stranger. I got paranoid. Paranoid enough that I decided to
fly to Seattle. Although I'd watched every episode of *Frasier*,
I'd never been to Seattle. I didn't know anyone who lived
there. Using money that I saved up while working at the
Chronicle, I booked my first-ever plane ticket, reserved my
very first hotel room, and asked Patricia if we could meet in
person. I don't remember exactly what we discussed while
sitting across from each other at the 13 Coins diner, not too
far from the *Times* office. Seventeen years later, she doesn't
remember much, either. But what I do remember was that
I wanted to look her in the eye, to show that I was a real
person. I didn't ask her to keep my secret. Nevertheless, she
didn't tell anyone about it.

After what happened with the *Times*, I was crushed. Rich
and Jim, whose scholarship sent me to college, suggested I meet
with an immigration lawyer. Jim covered the cost, and Rich
accompanied me to the meeting in downtown San Francisco.

The meeting did not go well. The only solution for me,
the lawyer said, was to leave the U.S., go back to the Philippines, and accept what's called a "10-year bar" before trying
to come back to America, this time legally. The moment the
lawyer said it, I was certain that it was the only solution. I
hadn't seen Mama for almost ten years. Maybe it was time to

go back, even if going back meant discarding what I'd done to build a life for myself here. I was so distraught at the thought of leaving that I didn't say a thing. In my mind, I was already starting to plan my trip back to Manila.

As we walked down Montgomery Street, looking for his parked car, Rich broke the silence.

"You're not going anywhere. You're already here," Rich said. "Put this problem on a shelf. Compartmentalize it. Keep going."

I'm not sure where my life would have gone without those words. I pocketed and referenced them whenever any kind of doubt surfaced. *Put this problem on a shelf. Compartmentalize it. Keep going.*

So I did. The following summer, I applied for the internship program at eight newspapers, including the *Chicago Tribune,* the *Boston Globe,* and the *Washington Post.* To my surprise—and it *was* a surprise—I was accepted by all of them, including the *Post.* I didn't think I had much of a chance given how competitive it was. But I landed one of the twenty available spots. I got it! After Cheryl Butler, the recruiter, called to offer me the internship, I emailed myself notes from our conversation, just to make sure I had not imagined it. Dated Wednesday, December 4, 2002, and time-stamped at 4:30 P.M., my notes read:

Cheryl Butler called and offered me the Metro desk internship at the Washington Post.

She said I'll be getting the Post for free for a month; someone will call about drug testing.

I should send a big picture; someone will call about housing.

I still can't believe it. I still can't believe it. I'm
still pinching myself, waiting for Cheryl to call back
and say, "Ooh, just kidding."
Well, well, Jose. Be proud, and stop being so paranoid.

Then the first person I called was Pat.

"Am I taking someone else's spot?" I asked. I always
thought I was taking someone else's spot. I had internalized
this anxiety from years of hearing the they're-taking-our-jobs
narrative about "illegals."

She cackled.

"Don't be ridiculous," she said. "You earned it. Go."

But going meant needing a driver's license. Unlike in
Philadelphia, where a license was not required, Cheryl, the
recruiter, reminded me that I needed a license to get the job.

7.

White People

Shortly after the holidays in 2003, I spent ten hours in the computer room at Mountain View's public library figuring out how to get a driver's license.

I googled every single state to find out their requirements. Each required a green card or a passport. Well, every state but Oregon. All Oregon required was a school ID, a birth certificate, and a proof of residency in Oregon. As luck would have it, Karen Willemsen, my former co-worker at the *Voice,* who was like a big sister to me, knew someone who lived in Portland, Oregon: Craig Walker, her father-in-law. Even though I'd never met Craig, he allowed me to use his mailing address as proof of residency. Along with a couple of close friends, I had Rich, Pat, and Mary send cards and letters to the Portland address. The most memorable card was from Mary, with a quote from someone named Tommy Lasorda on its cover: "The difference between the impossible and the possible lies in a person's determination." Inside, Mary wrote, "Jose, I love you. Mom."

Mary's son C.J., who was home in Mountain View, volunteered to drive me to Portland for my driving test. He was

attending trade school right outside Portland, and we made
the seven-hour drive in Mary's Jeep Grand Cherokee. Along
the way, C.J. and I stopped in Pioneer Square so I could practice parallel parking.

There was no failing this test. Weeks prior to my planned
trip to Portland, Rich would buy Starbucks and practice driving and parking with me in school parking lots. "The goal," he
said, "is to not make me spill this mocha on my lap."

In all those years I'd gotten closer to my second family,
I never introduced Lolo to Rich, Pat, or Mary. Lolo disap-
proved of me going to the *Post*. Working in San Francisco was
one thing; working in Washington, D.C., was a whole other
thing. In Lolo's mind, I was risking too much.

"Hindi ka dapat nandito," Lolo would say. ("You are not
supposed to be here.")

"Paano kung nahuli ka?" Lolo would ask. ("What if you
get caught?")

I scored 71 on the driving test. A passing score was 70.
My driver's license was issued on June 4, 2003, less than two
weeks before my internship at the *Post* began. It would expire
on February 3, 2011, the exact date of my thirtieth birthday.
This Oregon license would be my only piece of government-
issued identification for eight years. Meaning, I had eight
years to "earn" being a "citizen."

When I look back now, I am stunned that not one person
during that entire period wondered if we were doing the right
thing. There was a part of me that expected someone—maybe
Rich, maybe Mary—to ask: "Are we breaking the law here?"
Not once did someone say, "Wait, let's pause, let's think this
through, this may get sticky." Not once.

Recently, after meeting some members of my "white family," which is what I call the folks from Mountain View High School, a Mexican American friend asked me why I think all those white people helped me. Was it "white guilt"? The "white savior" thing? I laughed out loud. It's neither of those. I told him that even though I know that they're all white—physically, that is—I didn't think of them as white people when I was growing up. I associated white people with people who make you feel inferior, people who condescend to you, people who question why you are the way you are without acknowledging that you, too, are a human being with the same needs and wants.

I told my friend: "I didn't meet the kind of white people you're talking about—the people who put you in your place—until I moved to Washington, D.C."

8.

The *Washington Post*

My summer internship at the *Washington Post* led to a two-year internship out of college, which meant moving to Washington. Pat, Rich, Sheri, Mary, and Jim were thrilled. To them, there was no question that I should go. I'll never forget the pride in Rich's voice on the phone: "Jose, it's the *Washington Post*. It's *All the President's Men*. This is amazing."

Lolo continued to be against my going. He'd never heard of the *Post;* he'd never seen *All the President's Men*. On top of his litany of discouragement and disapproval—*"Hindi ka dapat nandito"* ("You are not supposed to be here") and *"Paano kung nahuli ka?"* ("What if you get caught?")—he added a new one: *"Masyado mong sinusugal ang buhay mo."* ("You are gambling with your life too much.") At that moment I realized that he feared for me, that it worried him that neither he nor I had any idea what could happen. Without ever saying it, he knew that I knew that I was here because of him, because of his lies, which were now my lies.

I had two graduation parties before moving to D.C. One was organized by Pat, Rich, Sheri, Mary, and Jim, and the other was planned by Lolo and Lola.

When I arrived at the *Post* on June 2, 2004, I knew I had to do everything I could to be "successful." In addition to the constant deadlines of newspaper reporting, there was a bigger personal deadline: February 3, 2011, the date my license would expire. It was a delicate dance: standing out in a highly competitive newsroom but not standing out so much as to draw attention and attract unwanted scrutiny. There was no room for error; I could not make any mistakes. There was also no room for enemies. I had to make friends and allies, but I had to make sure I didn't get too close to anyone or share more information than needed. I had to be careful.

I started freaking out about four months into the job, getting paranoid to the point of paralysis. It was one thing to risk being undocumented at the *San Francisco Chronicle*. It was a whole other thing to be undocumented at the *Washington Post,* hiding in plain sight in the nation's capital, where immigration was a constant topic of conversation. I was nervous, and it showed.

Over a lunch meeting with Deborah Heard, the editor in charge of the department I was working for, I was so obviously dripping with anxiety—about how I was performing, about whether my internship would lead to a permanent job—that she couldn't help but ask, "What could we do to not have you worry?"

During my first few months at the *Post,* I felt like a walking time bomb. Worse, only I could hear the ticking, which was nonstop, especially in a post-9/11 nation's capital that was swarming with security, where almost every professional you meet tries to figure out who you are, how you got there, and what they can use you for. I was wrapped in so much paranoia that I thought the phallic Washington Monument, which overlooks the whole city, was following me around, poking at me, daring me to slip and get found out. I never visited any of the free museums, telling myself that they didn't belong to me, that they were not for me to enjoy, that I was unwelcome in this city.

As the days and weeks passed, I walked around the newsroom like I had the word "ILLEGAL" tattooed on my forehead. It was getting harder and harder to focus on the work, and it became clear that I had to either leave the *Post* or find someone reliable who would keep my secret. As the years passed, as I kept on passing as an American, sharing my story was a compulsion, a way of relieving myself of the burden of the lies I had to tell so I could exist.

When I got back to my desk after lunch on October 27, 2004, I started looking at the website of the *Globe and Mail,* a newspaper in Canada. I had read that Canada had a friendlier immigration policy. Perhaps it was time to leave. After all, I can be a journalist anywhere in the world, I reassured myself. Maybe I was risking too much, as Lolo had warned. I couldn't just compartmentalize what I was feeling, as Rich had suggested two years before. Now was the time to tell somebody I could trust, in the same way I trusted Mrs. Denny, and Pat and Rich.

In my years of reporting, I'd developed a good sense of people, needing to size up potential sources quickly, whom to trust and whom to stay away from. Using the *Post*'s internal messaging system, I pinged Peter Perl, a longtime reporter who had recently been promoted to director of newsroom training and professional department.

> VARGASJ 10/27/2004 1:58:48 PM: are you here today, peter?
>
> PERLP 10/27/2004 2:37:49 PM: hi . . . i just got back & am here, till about 6. feel free to stop over. . . .
>
> VARGASJ 10/27/2004 2:38:40 PM: are you glued to your desk, or can i buy you starbucks? (i can afford it.) i have something important to tell you
>
> PERLP 10/27/2004 2:39:17 PM: please come visit . . . we can take a walk if we need to . . .

I first met Peter when I was a summer intern. Every intern was randomly assigned a "professional partner"—a mentor— and he was mine. Peter started working at the *Post* in 1981, the year I was born. Bob Woodward hired him from the *Providence Journal*. When I was selected for the two-year internship, Peter was among the first Posties, as *Post* employees were known, to send a note of congratulations.

Sitting on a bench in Lafayette Square, across from the White House, I told Peter about everything. All of it. The license I wasn't supposed to get. The fake green card. The help I got from Pat, Rich, Mary, and Jim. I told Peter that years ago, after I found out I was here illegally, Lolo took me to the local Social Security Administration office to apply for a Social Security number, which I needed if I was to get any kind of job. To apply, we used a fake passport with my name on it that Lolo had bought. When the Social Security card arrived, it clearly stated: "Valid for work only with I.N.S. authorization." Lolo took me to a nearby Kinko's. He covered the "I.N.S. authorization" text with a sliver of white tape, and we made twenty or so photocopies of the doctored card. That photocopied, doctored card, I told Peter, is what I had submitted to the *Post*'s human resources department.

After my disclosure, I expected Peter to say that we had to go to the human resources department. I braced myself.

"I understand you a hundred times better now," Peter said. "This is now our shared problem."

Peter said that I had done the right thing by telling him, and that he didn't want to do anything about it just yet. I had just been hired, he said, and I needed to prove myself. "When you've done enough," he said, "we'll tell Don and Len together." (Don Graham was the chairman of the Washington Post Company; Len Downie was the paper's executive editor.)

A month later, I spent my first Thanksgiving in Washington with Peter, his wife, Nina Shapiro, and their sons, Matt and Daniel. To my surprise, the generosity of strangers that I'd been fortunate to find at Mountain View High School extended nearly three thousand miles to the Shapiro-Perl household in Silver Spring, Maryland.

9.

Strangers

There is no passing alone.

At every challenging, complicated, and complicating juncture of my life—getting to college, getting a job, getting a driver's license so I could have a valid proof of identification so I could get a job, keeping the job—a stranger who did not remain a stranger saved me.

I use that word deliberately, because that was what each of them did, even if they didn't know what they were doing.

Saved.

They saved me.

After telling me that my green card was fake, the curly-haired, bespectacled woman at the DMV could have called immigration officials.

After finding out that I was ineligible for financial aid because I don't have any legal papers, the administrators, teachers, and parents at Mountain View High School didn't need to help me. I didn't even ask them for help, because I didn't know how to. But they offered help, even when I didn't know what kind of help I needed, even when they didn't know what they were doing.

After discovering that I was ineligible for a summer internship, the recruiter could have reported me to someone.

After I confessed about the fake papers, the doctored Social Security card, the driver's license I wasn't supposed to have, the senior newsroom personnel could have dragged me to the office of human resources and gotten me fired.

I don't know why they did what they did.

But I know for sure that all these Americans—all these strangers, all across the country—have allowed people like me to pass.

If just five people—a friend, a co-worker, a classmate, a neighbor, a faith leader—helped one of the estimated 11 million undocumented people in our country, then illegal immigration as we know it would touch at least 66 million people.

10.

Bylines

Being a reporter wasn't just a job. It was my entire identity. Journalism provided the framework for my life. I marked time by what story I was with struggling with (either the reporting or the writing or both), and which deadline for which article was looming. I was always on some kind of deadline for work, which made me sometimes forget about my other deadline: the expiration of my only piece of identification in a town that runs on business cards, résumés, and IDs.

Since the beginning of my journalism career, there was no escaping the fact that I was lying about myself so I could survive in a profession dependent on truth-telling. After decades of internalizing the dominant, nagging narrative that "illegals are taking our jobs," I couldn't stop myself from thinking that I was taking another person's livelihood. One way I reconciled the lies I told about myself was by taking my work very seriously: getting every fact right, insisting on context, telling the truth as much as the truth could be ascertained. I may lie about my status as an undocumented worker, but my work is true. I dealt with the notion that I took a job that could have gone to another journalist by writing stories that no other reporter could write.

When I was promoted to a full-time reporting job at the *Chronicle*, I was assigned to cover "diversity issues"—a code phrase for people of color in the *Chronicle*'s mostly white newsroom. But instead of writing about blacks, Latinos, and Asians, I decided to write about white people, particularly because the Bay Area was among the first minority-majority regions in the country. "In a world of racial diversity, what is 'white'? Caucasian students seek to define their culture, heritage," read the headline of a front page story I wrote that made top editors, all of whom were white, nervous. My direct editor, Pati Navalta, a Filipina American who was one of the few women-of-color editors in the newsroom, fought for the story. The article told the story of Justine Steele, a blond-haired, blue-eyed student who attended a high school of 4,054 people of whom 8 percent were white. I began the story with this lede: "The other students call her 'white girl.'"

"You could get away with that story because of your byline," one of the senior editors, a white woman who was friendly with me, said after the story was published. "Your byline doesn't sound white or black." She sounded like Mrs. Wakefield after the O.J. Simpson trial.

I convinced myself that I could also come up with original story ideas when I got to the *Post*. No one else, I told myself, can do what I do. Though it sounds self-important, delusional, and unrealistic, it was my way of arriving at some sort of peace so I could do my work.

I lived alone, in a small studio that was less than three blocks from the newsroom. I didn't have too many friends outside work, and even then, I did not spend too much time outside work. I was so overwhelmed with all the reporting, writing, and revising that I had to do that I kept a pillow under my desk in case I needed to take naps. Though I was a solid reporter, I was a relatively weak writer. In my early years of news reporting, I was so insecure about my English that I sometimes wrote my first drafts in Tagalog before translating them in English. I had to work extra hard to make sure my copy was clean enough, especially in an institution that prided itself on being a "writer's newspaper."

Assigned to the Style section, the *Post*'s storied feature section, I wrote about the culture of video games and began reporting deeply on the HIV/AIDS epidemic in D.C. My reporting on AIDS led to a yearlong series of stories chronicling the epidemic in the District, while my front-page articles on video games caught the eye of some top editors. David Hoffman, the genial editor of the foreign desk, asked me out to lunch one afternoon, days after I wrote a story about video games being the rock and roll of the war in Iraq. Over burgers at Bobby Van's, a steakhouse near the office, he asked me if I was interested in going to Baghdad to write what he called "Jose stories," which, in my mind, meant stories about technology culture, and youth culture. He said he could see me as a foreign correspondent.

I excused myself and headed to the bathroom. How do I turn this opportunity down without sounding suspicious? I didn't have a cell phone and couldn't call Peter or Rich or Pat to ask for advice.

When I got back to the table, the only thing I could say that was not a barefaced lie was: "I grew up overseas."

"I'm not really looking to travel internationally," I added. "I want to get to know America more."

David looked perplexed. In the friendliest way he could, he said that if I wanted to rise through the ranks at the *Post,* I should consider being a foreign correspondent or a political reporter.

The moment he said that, I jumped. "I want to be a political reporter."

I had little experience covering politics. Yes, I covered city hall meetings when I was at the *Voice* and helped cover the California gubernatorial recall election when I was at the *Chronicle.* But this was national politics, and this was the *Post,* the home of the Watergate investigation, a news organization whose bread and butter is politics. There were older, much better, and more experienced reporters at the *Post* waiting their turn to be national political reporters. I figured the only way I would ever cover politics was if I came up with a beat that no one else had.

Like all newspapers, the *Post* struggled to adapt to the digital era, a deficit that I used to my advantage. I wanted to use online videos to accompany my feature stories, going as far as learning how to shoot and edit videos myself on my own time. At the time, the print newsroom, which was in Washington, was separate from the digital newsroom, which was across the river in Virginia. I had to go to Virginia to figure out how to "package" my feature stories with videos. Some of my colleagues scoffed at my efforts at what was being called multimedia journalism. Others were supportive. Nevertheless, using technology was a way to stand out in a newsroom that was struggling to figure out how to leverage it.

Technology was also my ticket to being a political reporter. Most political reporters had enough trouble adjusting to their BlackBerrys, much less understanding what social media was. After watching Hillary Clinton announce that she was running for president in an online video—"I'm beginning a conversation, with you, with America," she said—I wrote a two-page memo pitching a new area of coverage: the marriage of politics and technology. The 2008 campaign, I argued in the memo, will be the first digital-powered, social-networking-oriented presidential race. Since I had a Facebook account and knew what YouTube was (Twitter had yet to break at the time), I said that I was uniquely suited for this beat and outlined several areas of coverage. Instead of sending the memo to my editor, who would then have to send it to her editor, and then her editor to his or her editor, I sent the memo directly to the *Post*'s top two editors: Len Downie and Philip Bennett. Bennett called me into his office, and less than two weeks later, I was put on the campaign team.

The editors I bypassed were irked, to say the least. I apologized, because I had to and because I meant it. I told one that, if I had sent the memo to her, I didn't think I would have gotten the chance to cover politics. *Not enough experience. Too young. Wait your turn.* What I did not tell that editor, or any other editors, was that I had a personal deadline. Looking back now, I must have been a frustrating reporter to manage. My ambition far outweighed my skills. I was trying to sprint in a marathon.

Lynne Duke, a reporter-turned-editor, was one of the senior Posties who took me under her wing. Lynne was among several black women at the *Post*—in addition to Marcia Davis, my editor, and her boss, Deborah, there was Vanessa Williams, Teresa Wiltz, Robin Givhan, et al.—who formed a kind of sisterhood: they championed one another, and, for some reason, they all ended up guiding me in some way.

The first time I heard from Lynne was when she read an extensive profile I wrote on a longtime community activist. "That piece was good. Until the end. Your kicker"—the ending sentence or paragraph of a story—"ruined it," she told me. I disagreed, but I cherished her brand of tough-love. Over lunch near the office one afternoon soon after I was promoted as a political reporter, after I told her all my ideas for coverage, she said: "Jose, you need to understand what kind of journalist you're going to be before the political machine eats you up. Because it will eat you up."

Then and there I wanted to tell Lynne what was eating me up.

But I stopped myself.

I wasn't prepared for whatever her reaction would be.

11.
Campaign 2008

"Young man," the sheriff said as he leaned against my rental car. "Did you know you were driving about thirty miles over the speed limit?" He took off his sunglasses. "License and registration, please."

It was March 2008. This was the first time I was pulled over by any kind of law enforcement. Usually, I was more than cautious, driving at or below the speed limit. But I was on deadline on an election night, and I did not realize I was driving that fast. And of all the places to get caught, I was pulled over in Texas, where I'd been driving for the past two weeks covering the historic primary race between Barack Obama and Hillary Clinton. As I slowly reached for my license, questions ricocheted in my head. What if the sheriff finds out that I'm not supposed to have this license? What if he puts me through some test and I forget the address that's listed on the license? If he calls immigration on me, if I get arrested on the spot, do I get a phone call? What do I tell Lynne Duke, my editor, who is waiting on me to file a story, which was already late?

The sheriff's cell phone rang.

As he walked away from my car to answer the call, I felt something wet trickling down in my pants.

I had peed myself.

"I gotta head back to the station," the sheriff said. "I'm gonna let you go. Slow down, young man."

Slow down.

I had more than one deadline.

There was no slowing down.

I froze as he drove away as the stench of urine filled the car. Since procuring a license I wasn't supposed to have, driving had always been stressful. One way I dealt with the tension was by playing Stevie Wonder's "Don't You Worry 'Bout a Thing," which turned out to be the soundtrack of the two years I traveled the country covering the 2008 campaign. I drove all over the early voting states of Iowa and New Hampshire, got lost in Kentucky while following John Edwards, and got even more lost in Indiana while covering Sarah Palin. I got lost trying to follow Oprah Winfrey in South Carolina, where she was campaigning for Barack Obama. I was witnessing and covering history yet I felt so removed from it, like I had no right to be there.

Driving down Highway 175 that night in Texas, as Stevie was reminding me not to worry about a thing, I couldn't help but worry about everything.

Even when it seemed like everything was going well, really well, I worried about everything.

12.

Purgatory

"Jose! My man! Congratulations, you won!" Kevin Merida, one of the *Post*'s top editors, called to tell me the good news.

I was confused. Won what, I wondered? According to Kevin, I won, as part of a team, the Pulitzer Prize for breaking news reporting for covering the 2007 Virginia Tech massacre. My contribution to the winning package was an interview with a key eyewitness, whom I reached because I knew how to use Facebook. I didn't believe I had won anything until I saw my byline in the package; even then, I didn't really believe it until I saw my name listed in the nominating letter to the Pulitzer committee.

But instead of feeling elated, the first thing that crossed my mind was: What if anybody finds out?

A couple of hours later, as news of the prize spread—not only in the U.S. but in the Philippines, where news reports said I was the youngest and only the fourth Filipino journalist to win—my phone rang. It was my grandmother. It was Lola. She didn't say congratulations, or say how proud she was of me, or ask me how I felt. She was worried about what I was worrying about. Spoken in a whisper that dripped with shame, Lola asked: *"Anong mangyayari kung malaman ng mga tao?"* ("What will happen if people find out?")

I ignored the question. I told her I had to go. After I hung up, I rushed to the bathroom on the fourth floor of the newsroom. I sat down on the toilet. I cried.

In a way, winning a part of the prize was the beginning of the end. The lies had gotten so big that they swallowed everything up, including all the good things. The lies, I remember thinking that day, had to stop. I didn't exactly know how to stop them or when to stop them or what I would do after I stopped them. I just knew that they had to stop.

Passing was purgatory. It was exhausting, always looking over your shoulder, waiting to get found out, always wondering if you're not passing enough. Paranoia was like some viral disease that infected my whole body. Stress was oxygen.

I couldn't be present for my own life. Even—no, especially—on a day like this.

13.
Thirty

Reading *The New Yorker* felt like shopping at a grocery store for food I'd never tasted and probably could not afford. I told myself then, improbable as it sounds: if I'm ever going to be a serious writer—whatever that means—I need to write for this thing. And then I got my chance.

"Where are you from?" Mark Zuckerberg wanted to know.

We were walking around his leafy neighborhood, not too far from the headquarters of Facebook. It was a sunny, cloudless afternoon. I was getting to know him; he was, in turn, getting to know me. Zuckerberg was not the awkward, Asperger-y type that he had been portrayed to be. He looked me in the eye. Minutes after we were introduced, he was texting with his mother. I requested that he and I take an hour-long stroll, just a reporter and his subject, speaking on the record, no holds barred. Zuckerberg, often flanked by his handlers whenever he talked to reporters, agreed to the walk. It was August 6, 2010, and I was living a dream—a big part of my dream.

I was on an assignment for *The New Yorker,* one of the

magazines I had discovered at the local library when I was a kid. I was mystified by the black-and-white cartoons (were they supposed to be funny?), confused by the punctuation marks (I thought a semicolon was a mistake; it looked like a period on top of a comma), and needed a dictionary and an encyclopedia to digest a lengthy review of a new book on Shakespeare. Not only that, but I had beaten more experienced and, frankly, better writers and landed an exclusive interview with a largely misunderstood and often caricatured character: Zuckerberg, the founder and CEO of Facebook, who, at the time, had yet to be deeply profiled. The profile would come out before the premiere of *The Social Network*. I had convinced Zuckerberg and his trusted team, including Sheryl Sandberg, that I was the right journalist for the job. Unlike most reporters, I told Sheryl, I actually knew how to use Facebook. I had assured *The New Yorker*, eager for the exclusive, that I was a fair journalist for the job. ("Are you sure you're not 'friends-friends' with Mark?" David Remnick, the magazine's top editor, asked me.) Zuckerberg was twenty-six. I was twenty-nine, about six months shy of turning thirty.

Turning thirty weighs heavily on most people, who think they should be married by then or should be making a certain amount of money. It weighed heavily on me for reasons I could not share with even my closest friends, much less my mentors and previous employers, including Arianna Huffington, who recruited me to join the *Huffington Post* in the summer of 2009, and Donald Graham, the former owner of the Washington Post Company, where I was hired right after college. (As it happened, Graham had introduced me to Zuckerberg at the White House Correspondents' Dinner in

2007. "Oh, you're not wearing flip-flops," were my first words to Zuckerberg.) By the summer of 2010, at the peak of my journalism career, depression had completely sunk in. Worse, I refused to share what troubled me for fear of drawing people into a kind of a tempest I myself did not fully comprehend. All I knew was, turning thirty came with a deadline, both practical and personal.

Practically, my driver's license—the only legal form of identification I had—was set to expire on February 3, 2011, my thirtieth birthday.

Personally, I had hoped that, by the dawn of my fourth decade, life, the kind of life that did not mean hiding from the government, hiding from loved ones, even hiding from myself—real life—would actually begin.

"I'm from Mountain View," I replied.

It was the easy answer to Zuckerberg's easy question, the kind of question I had never fully answered since I found out that I was not supposed to be here. I never answered it fully on government forms, be it while applying for jobs or a driver's license. I rarely answered it fully when friends, coworkers, and even potential lovers inquired about why I had not visited my mother or why I rarely talked about her, or why my grandparents raised me, or why I couldn't take advantage of an all-expense-paid trip to Switzerland, or why I didn't want to work in Baghdad and cover the war in Iraq.

Journalism was a way of separating what I do from who I am, a way of justifying my compromised, unlawful existence to myself: *My name may be at the top of this story, I may have done all the reporting and the writing, but I'm not even supposed to be here, so I'm not really here.*

Since I began writing, the three most dangerous words in the English language for me have been "I," "me," and "my." That's partly because I've so internalized the axiom that I need to "earn" my American citizenship that I'm uncertain if I've "earned" the right to express myself in such personal terms. It's also partly because I'm afraid of what happens when I confront my own despair, the sense of disorientation and abandonment I've been grappling with since arriving in this country as a motherless twelve-year-old. I run away from people, especially people who want to get close. I run away from myself. Because I've never felt at home, because I've never had a real home, I've organized my life so I'm constantly on the move and on the go, existing everywhere and nowhere. I cannot sit still. I live at airports, which is somewhat fitting, since my life was changed that one morning in an airport in a country I left to go to a country where I've built a life that I have not been able to leave.

14.

Facing Myself

My relationships with people were shaped by the secrets I kept and the lies I had to tell; I feared that the more I shared of myself, the more people I would drag into my mess.

The lies I told to get jobs were exacerbated by the lies I told friends and coworkers about who I was, where I came from, what I could not do, and why.

When my friend Angelica invited me to her wedding in Mexico City, I made up some lie about my grandmother being sick. For me, traveling outside of the country was out of the question. If I leave the U.S., there's no guarantee I would be allowed back.

I never displayed photos of family members at work or at home. You put photos up, people ask questions.

There were many times I actually told people that my parents were dead. It was easier to say that I was alone, just as, years earlier, it was easier for me to represent myself at parent-teacher meetings.

For more than a decade, I carried the weight of trying to succeed in my profession—I need that byline, I need that

story, I need to be seen—while wanting to be invisible so I
didn't draw too much attention to myself.

Then came the Zuckerberg story. There I was, walking
down California Avenue, near downtown Palo Alto, less than
two miles from the home where I was raised, cajoling Zuckerberg to open up to me (I had asked him about his trip to
an ashram in India; about his mistakes and regrets running
Facebook at such a young age; about his controversial views
on transparency and publicness), while unable to truly open
up about myself. Throughout 2010, I started reading stories
about young undocumented Americans, many of them still
in high school and college. Their rallying cry was: "We're undocumented, unafraid, and unapologetic." And using new
technologies that I'd been writing about—Facebook, Twitter, YouTube—they were chronicling their own stories, daring
politicians and the public alike to look away. I was particularly attracted to the story of a young undocumented immigrant from Ecuador named Maria Gabriela Pacheco, whom
everyone called Gaby. She had been organizing for immigrant
rights since she was in high school. Joined by three friends,
Gaby walked from Miami, where she grew up, to Washington
to drum up support for the DREAM Act. I followed Gaby's
story on social media. I even stalked her on Facebook. There
she was in the news, sharing her story publicly and trying
to engage people like Joe Arpaio, the notorious sheriff who
talked about and treated undocumented immigrants like cattle. How could she be so fearless? Why was I so scared?

There comes a moment in each of our lives when we must
confront the central truth in order for life to go on.

For my life to go on, I had to get at the truth about where

I came from. On that August afternoon, working on the biggest assignment of my life, I realized that I could no longer live with the easy answer. I could no longer live with my lies. Passing was no longer enough. Before I could write any more stories, I had to investigate my life.

To free myself—in fact, to face myself—I had to write my story.

15.

Lawyers

I had spoken with at least ten immigration lawyers, all of whom told me that telling my full story publicly was not a good idea. One lawyer went as far as calling it "legal suicide." Talking to lawyers made me feel like I was carrying an incurable disease, with everyone offering their diagnoses. Few offered treatments.

"The thing is, you weren't supposed to make it this far," a lawyer told me as she sipped a Diet Coke.

One warned, "The moment you publicly declare that you're undocumented, you cannot get hired. How are you going to make a living?"

Another had an interesting suggestion that kept me sleepless for a few nights: "What if you left the country and came out as undocumented from the Philippines?"

Given my high-profile contacts, one lawyer wondered if I had considered asking a member of Congress to introduce a private bill, typically a last-ditch effort to protect immigrants from deportation. "Having a senator introduce a private bill on your behalf—even if it doesn't pass, because they rarely pass—offers you a safety net." I told her that I would consider it. But the whole point of my planning to come out as un-documented was to marry my specific story to other stories. To complicate the narrative. To take immigration, especially unauthorized, "illegal" immigration, out of the "merit-based," "good immigrant v. bad immigrant," "less deserving v. more deserving" framework.

"Are you trying to be a martyr?" she asked.

"No," I replied. "I am trying to be a human being."

I kept thinking back to that lawyer sipping the Diet Coke: "You weren't supposed to make it this far."

But because I am here, because I did make it this far, because of the sacrifices of Mama, Lolo, and Lola, and in spite of their fear and shame, because I could not have done what I've done without the love and support of strangers who became mentors and allies, because of all of that, I have an even greater responsibility to speak up. Many of us hold some kind of privilege. It was time for me to risk mine.

16.
Second Coming Out

About "coming out," which I've done twice in my life: it's less about "coming out" and more about letting people in. I learned that you come out to let people in. The reality is, the closet doesn't only hide you from strangers. The closet also hides you from the people you love.

For more than a decade, I hid my Filipino family from my "white" family of mentors and allies, and I hid my friends from both of them. It was easier to keep everyone apart.

Many members of my Filipino family did not know (or did not want to know) that I was gay. Most of my closest friends did not know that I was undocumented. I compartmentalized people like I compartmentalized feelings.

To celebrate my thirtieth birthday, the day my driver's license from Oregon was set to expire, I decided it was time for everyone to meet everyone. I threw myself an "I may get deported" party to share my decision to come out as undocumented, with the goal of sparking a more honest, more inclusive conversation about immigration and the millions of people many Americans deem "illegal." In front of everyone I loved, I said that I was not sure what would happen to me—

arrest? detention? deportation?—but what I did know was that I needed all of them to know each other.

Most people in the room had an idea of what I was planning on doing. That night, many of them told me they didn't really believe it until I shared it in front of the whole group.

"I was hoping you'd change your mind," my friend Scott told me.

Thirty people showed up, traveling in from all over the country. With the help of my aunt Jennifer, I had organized a dinner at an Indian restaurant in downtown San Francisco. Lola came, accompanied by Uncle Rolan, his wife, Alma, and their children A.J. and Nicole. Lolo's sister Florida attended, as did several aunts, uncles, and cousins, including Aida, my exuberant aunt, and Ate Gladys, a cousin who's more like the older sister I never had. All my mentors from Mountain View High School showed up. After meeting Pat, Rich, Sheri, Mary, Daisy, and Jim for the first time, Lola turned to me and said, *"Hindi ko alam na puti pala silang lahat."* ("I didn't know that they were all white.") Beloved friends from New York City and Washington, D.C., made the trip. My reporting career has been guided by editors who became mentors and later very dear friends. It was a special thrill to introduce Teresa Moore, the editor who helped get me a job at the *Chronicle*, to Marcia Davis, who edited most of my work at the *Post*.

As people mingled with each other through the buffet dinner of chicken curry, samosas, biryani, and naan, I realized that I had made a mistake by keeping everyone apart all these years. I was afraid that they wouldn't have anything to talk about. It was not until my family life, my school life, and my work life all converged in that Indian restaurant that I discovered that they indeed had something in common: their generosity to me.

And to be seen by so many people, so many good people, meant that I was here, and maybe even that I was supposed to be here.

Uncle Conrad, who flew in from San Diego, pulled me aside and told me he was overwhelmed after meeting everyone.

"Your whole life is here," he said.

Not my whole life. Lolo had been gone for four years. He died of a heart attack in January 2007. I was glad that we were able to reconcile months before he died, to get to an understanding about why he did what he did and why I did what I had to do. I apologized for all the hurtful things I said. I apologized for being rebellious and disobedient, for running away from him, thinking that he resented whatever it was I had become. Turns out, he didn't resent it—he just didn't understand it.

"Hindi ko alam na mangayayari ang lahat ng ito, apo ko." ("I didn't know all of this would happen, my grandson.")

Lolo wasn't the only major figure in my life who was absent from the party. Two months after we buried Lolo, my father, whom I hadn't seen since I was about eleven years old, was dying from lung cancer. I found out when his siblings found a way to contact me, first by email and then by phone. They needed help in paying for my father's funeral. At first I didn't know what to do. I was angry. And I was angry that I was angry. When the anger subsided, the only appropriate thing to do was to send whatever extra money I had to the man who was partly responsible for my being born.

17.
Outlaw

I was about to throw away the career that I'd risked every-thing for. No one was forcing me to do it. I was forcing myself to do it.

After *The New Yorker* published a profile I'd written head-lined "Mark Zuckerberg Opens Up"—and four months after hosting my "I may get deported" birthday party for my family and friends—it was my turn to open up.

On June 22, 2011, the *New York Times Magazine* pub-lished "My Life as an Undocumented Immigrant." The essay's other headline: "OUTLAW."

The moment my forty-three-hundred-word confessional was posted online, Define American was born. Cofounded with a close group of friends (Jake Brewer, one of the early innovators in online advocacy and organizing; Jehmu Greene, the former head of nonprofit groups Rock the Vote and Women's Media Center; and Alicia Menendez, a journalist and policy expert who knew more about the ins and outs of immigration than Jake, Jehmu, and I combined did), Define American is unlike anything else in the immigrant rights space. Our tactics, from the outset, have focused on neither policy nor politics. Taking a page from the playbook of the LGBTQ rights movement, we believe that you cannot change the politics of immigration until you change the culture in which immigrants are seen. Storytelling is central to our strategy: collecting stories of immigrants from all walks of life, creating original content (documentaries, databases, graphics, etc.), and leveraging stories we've collected and stories we've told to influence how news and entertainment media portray immigrants, both documented and undocumented. If you're a reporter looking for an undocumented mother who's taken sanctuary in a church, you can come to us. If you're a producer of a TV medical drama looking for stories of undocumented doctors to integrate in your show, you can contact us. Our #FactsMatter campaign combats every myth and answers every question you have about immigration. We have a #WordsMatter campaign that combats anti-immigrant speech and rhetoric that are rampant in all forms of media. Inspired by the Gay Straight Alliance movement, which grew around the time I came out as gay in high school, we started a chapters program whose members consist of undocumented students and their U.S. citizen classmates. There are almost 60 chapters in college campuses in 26 states plus D.C.

A couple of days before my essay was scheduled to be published, I was at the *Times* building in Manhattan, going over the printed proofs of the essay, double-checking every fact, rereading every sentence. Since I've lied about so many facts about my life so I could pass as an American, the last thing I needed was any kind of correction. The essay had to be airtight, unimpeachable.

My phone rang. It was one of the immigration lawyers

who had been advising me. As a courtesy, I had sent a copy of the essay to the lawyers.

"Jose, are you going to print that you've done things that are 'unlawful'? In the *New York Times*?"

"Yes. It's in the essay."

"Jose, the moment you publish that, we cannot help you."

"Jose, are you there?"

She took a big breath.

Telling the truth—admitting that I had lied on government forms to get jobs—meant that "getting legal" would be nearly impossible.

I took a big breath.

"If I can't admit that, then why am I doing this?"

Publishing the essay, I realized, was breaking a cardinal rule in journalism: *write* the story, don't *be* the story. And, for more than a decade, I had already broken another cardinal rule of journalism—lying. For the record, I never lied in any of my stories. I never fabricated a single fact or contextual detail or made up a source, lies that ended the careers of other journalists I'd heard and read about, from Janet Cooke to Stephen Glass to Jayson Blair. Still, I had lied about who I am, specifically my legal status, a defining element of my life. To get jobs, I had lied to employers, from the *Chronicle* to the *HuffPost,* about my citizenship status. The essay was meant to right that wrong, to trace the origins of those lies, an attempt at getting at the "how" and "why." Why did I have to lie? How does someone become "illegal"?

To me, writing the essay was a personal reckoning: tell the truth, don't pull any punches, legal ramifications be damned. Writing the essay was also a journalistic endeavor. Against the advice of lawyers—all of whom counseled me to not reveal this or that detail—I wrote it because I believed that its journalistic service to the public good was worth more than my personal need for legal protection. Yes, my life in this country was based on lies. Yes, I needed to pass as an American and as a U.S. citizen so I could work. But my journalism has always been grounded in truth since I covered that fire on the street I grew up on, and being a journalist is an identity I wear with deep pride. I'm such a child of newsrooms that I constructed the essay with other reporters in mind. I imagined their curiosity rising as they read certain details. "I was paying state and federal taxes, but I was using an invalid Social Security card and writing false information on my employment forms," I wrote in one part. In another part, I detailed how I got a driver's license from Oregon. In writing the essay, I thought I was leaving bread crumbs for journalists to follow and investigate the "why" and "how" of it all.

There are so many "how" questions.

How do undocumented workers who have no legal papers pay income taxes?

The government has no problem taking our money; it just won't recognize that we have the right to earn it. Using my doctored Social Security number (SSN), which is not valid for employment, I've paid income taxes since I started regularly working at eighteen. Many undocumented workers who don't have SSNs use ITINs. ITIN stands for Individual Taxpayer Identification Number, a tax processing number issued by the IRS. Regardless of immigration status, all wage earners are required to pay federal taxes. Nationwide, the amount of taxes that the Internal Revenue Service collects from undocumented workers ranges from almost $2.2 million in Montana, which has an estimated undocumented population of four thousand, to more than $3.1 billion in California, which is home to more than three million undocumented immigrants. According to the nonpartisan Institute on Taxation and Economic Policy, undocumented immigrants nationwide pay an estimated 8 percent of their incomes in state and local taxes on average. To put that in perspective, the top 1 percent of taxpayers pay an average nationwide effective tax rate of just 5.4 percent.

How do undocumented workers contribute to Social Security?

I'll never forget the day I received a letter from the Social Security Administration (SSA) outlining my "earnings record." The letter said that I'd paid $28,838 to Social Security and that my employer also paid $28,838. I didn't keep track of it. All I knew was, whenever I got a paycheck, they took out money for Social Security and Medicare. I never bothered wondering what that meant, given that I knew I had no access to the funds. Crazy as it sounds, since I wasn't even supposed to be working in the first place, I figured paying into the system and not benefiting from it was some kind of penance.

Perhaps a whole lot of workers are doing a whole lot of penance. According to the SSA itself, unauthorized workers have paid $100 billion into the fund over the past decade. An estimated seven million people are currently working in the U.S. illegally, of whom 3.1 million are using fake or expired Social Security numbers and also paying automatic payroll taxes. Exactly how the SSA accepts and credits payment to invalid accounts, I have no idea. Money always finds a way.

Annually, undocumented workers pay $12 billion to the Social Security Trust Fund.

The reality behind these numbers—the stories they tell about how undocumented people fit in the fabric of our society—is not reflected in the way the news media frames illegal immigration. Our country's mainstream news organizations often fail to report basic facts about how much undocumented workers pay into a government that vilifies us. Whether because of ignorance or indifference, or both, failure to report these facts and provide context has perpetuated the myth of the "illegal" who is taxing social services and taking away from "real Americans." Worse, the general ignorance and indifference by credible news outlets is dwarfed by conservative media that has prioritized immigration coverage to drive their fanatical followers to their content.

A longtime journalist who edited immigration for a regional news outlet told me: "Even when we report facts about undocumented immigrants, the readers either don't care or don't want to believe it. That's how successful the right-wing sites have been."

The overall result?

Immigrants are seen as mere labor, our physical bodies judged by perceptions of what we contribute, or what we take. Our existence is as broadly criminalized as it is commodified. I don't how many times I've explained to a fellow journalist that even though it is an illegal act to enter the country without documents, it is not illegal for a person to be in the country without documents. That is a clear and crucial distinction. I am not a criminal. This is not a crime.

Immediately after my essay was posted online and shared

on social media, I was viewed with suspicion, sometimes dismissed as an "advocate" with a "clear bias" and an obvious "agenda." My truth—the facts of how I got here, the context in which I had to lie in order to survive—was an agenda. I was no longer just writing the stories, I was now being written about, subject to how other people perceive the story based on their knowledge of the issue. I was prepared for that. I expected it. After all, journalists, especially the good ones, are known for their bullshit detectors. What I did not fully anticipate was that my story would be largely viewed through a political lens, usually couched and anatomized in partisan and politicized terms. Here's the "immigration reform," "pro-immigrant" side, and here's the "no amnesty," "anti-immigrant" side, substituting the appearance of balance and neutrality for real insight.

To achieve journalistic "objectivity," we sacrifice people's humanity. It was a sobering experience, being on the other side. It made me wonder how the subjects of and sources for my news stories felt about what I wrote.

A few months after I profiled Zuckerberg, I approached David Remnick, the editor of *The New Yorker*, about my story. I got him on the phone, confessed that I was undocumented, and said that I was planning to come out. I said I wanted to publish the essay in his magazine. He wasn't interested. I hung up.

Mustering some much-needed courage, I then reached out to Katharine Weymouth, the publisher of the *Washington Post*. Unlike Remnick, Weymouth was interested in the story. She connected me with Marcus Brauchli, the *Post*'s top editor. The last time I'd communicated with Brauchli was in the summer of 2009. I was still in the closet about my undocumented status, and he was trying to convince me to stay at the *Post*. Instead, I left to work for *HuffPost*.

Brauchli wondered if he could assign *Post* journalists to interview me and write my story. I declined. I insisted on writing the story myself. For three months I worked with Carlos Lozada, the editor of the Outlook section, which publishes op-eds and commentary. An immigrant from Peru, Carlos legally emigrated to the U.S. as a child. He was one of a handful of Latino editors in the entire newsroom. Carlos has a good bullshit detector. He was relentless in making sure I was telling the truth, the whole truth. While we were crafting the essay, Carlos wondered what form of identification I was using to get through airport security since my Oregon driver's license had expired. Following the advice of my lawyers, I hadn't told him that I managed to procure a new license from Washington State, one of the few states that allow its undocumented residents to drive. Carlos was adamant that we include that information in the essay. We did. Another editor, Ann Gerhart, also known for her keen journalistic eye, and an ace fact-checker, Julie Tate, rereported what I wrote, to make sure all the facts lined up. I was getting anxious about the essay's publication date when Carlos called to tell me that Brauchli decided to kill the story. Carlos did not agree with the decision; he urged me to find a home for the essay that he had meticulously edited for weeks. I emailed Brauchli and got no response. I emailed one of his deputies, Liz Spayd. Still, no response. I was floored. Hurt. This was the *Post,* where I'd grown up, to which I owe so much of my journalistic identity. But there was no time to feel anything. I needed a Plan B. I reached out to Peter Baker, a friend and former colleague at the *Post* who had decamped to the *Times*. Peter vouched for me. When Peter shared my essay with other editors at the *Times*, they rushed to publish it.

The *Post* ran a news story explaining why they spiked my essay. The headline: "Why did the *Post* deport Jose Antonio Vargas's story?"

Looking back to that summer of 2011, what some of my fellow journalists failed to grasp about my specific story represented the inability of the agenda-setting news media to understand the broader issue of immigration and the millions of people who are directly affected by it. This disconnect cannot be divorced from the fact that, in a country where the Latino population, the country's largest racial minority group, sits at more than fifty-eight million, journalists of Latin descent are grossly underrepresented in most major American newsrooms. That was the case when I was starting out in the late 1990s. It's still very much the case today. Of course, immigration is not only a Latino issue. But because immigration is often tied to race, Latinos are disproportionately affected.

To an undocumented immigrant who happens to be a journalist, what has made the past few years even more maddening is how generally uninformed journalists are about immigration. With some notable exceptions—including the insightful work by Dara Lind at *Vox* and Cindy Carcamo at the *Los Angeles Times*, not to mention Maria Hinojosa at NPR's *Latino USA*, Univision's Jorge Ramos, and the syndicated columnist Ruben Navarrette Jr., to name just a few—the mainstream media's coverage of immigration is lackluster at best and irresponsible at worst, promoting and sustaining stereotypes while spreading misinformation. Television is the worst culprit. Facts often take *facts vs politicians*

a backseat to what this or that political figure has to say about immigrants. Context is the invisible ghost that haunts many TV segments, radio hits, and news articles. Most journalists and media influencers I've spoken to or have been interviewed by do not know basic information about immigration and how the system works—or doesn't.

In the early days of Define American, our team fielded regular requests from MSNBC, CNN, and Fox News to talk about immigration. Usually the "live hits," as the segments are called, involved debating someone who is a Republican pundit or operative. Sometimes it would be with a Democrat, and the segment was billed as more of a conversation. Whatever the framing, the live hit would last somewhere between two and three minutes, if that, which means I would get no more than forty-five seconds, maybe a minute in total, if I was lucky, to make a point. Often, the issue would be about "comprehensive immigration reform," or "border security," or the DREAM Act, as if those were the only issues that concern undocumented immigrants in particular and Americans in general.

In February 2017, a month after President Trump took office, I agreed to go on Erin Burnett's eponymous show on CNN. The subject was Trump's plan to "secure the border." Before we went on-air, Erin turned to me and asked: "So, you're still undocumented, right?" I was flabbergasted. Did she think being undocumented is like some light that I can easily turn on or off?

Twice I've been a guest on HBO's *Real Time with Bill Maher*. There was a small reception for the guests and their guests after the live taping, and Maher showed up for a few minutes to mingle. At the reception after my second appearance, in April 2017, Maher told me he was confused. "I just don't understand," he said, "why you just can't fix this thing," as if "this thing" is a chipped tooth or a dent in a Tesla. If Maher, of all people, doesn't understand how even someone high profile like me can't just "fix this thing," then it shouldn't be a surprise that most people, regardless of political affiliation, have no idea how the immigration system works.

If Bill Maher doesn't get it, we're all in trouble.

When I found out that Chuck Todd, the host of NBC's *Meet the Press,* was scheduled to do a one-on-one interview with Donald Trump as he secured the Republican presidential nomination in May 2016, I emailed Todd and asked that we speak on the phone. On the call, I told him that Asians, not Latinos, are the fastest-growing undocumented population in the country and urged him to ask Trump how building a wall on the southern border would protect Americans from undocumented Asians who flew here and overstayed their visas. I added that, with nearly three-quarters of all Asian adults born abroad, Asians have passed Latinos as the largest group of new immigrants to the U.S.

"That's a good point," he said before we hung up. Then I emailed him an article from *The Atlantic.* "Asians Now Outpace Mexicans in Terms of Undocumented Growth—Chinese, South Koreans, and Indians Among the Fastest-Growing Segments of Undocumented Immigrants," the headline read. Todd never did ask my question, perhaps because it did not fit the narrative. Maybe he just ran out of time.

Collectively, the news media is running out of time in chronicling a demographic makeover unlike anything this country has ever seen. The estimated eleven million undocumented immigrants don't live on an island unto ourselves. At least forty-three million immigrants, documented and undocumented, reside in these United States. You cannot separate the documented from the undocumented population, because many undocumented people, myself included, have family members who are U.S. citizens or permanent legal residents. At least nine million people, in fact, are part of what are called "mixed-status" families—households in which one member or more is here legally and the others are not. We're all mixed up.

Race, class, and immigration are intertwined, utterly inseparable. Unlike the largely European immigrants of previous generations, most of today's immigrants hail from Asia and Latin America, the direct result of the 1965 Immigration and Nationality Act. Arguably the least-known yet most significant piece of legislation that changed the racial makeup of the country, the law was signed a year after the Civil Rights Act of 1964 and less than three months after the Voting Rights Act of 1965. The timeline is significant; without the racial consciousness ushered in by black Americans and their white allies during the civil rights movement, the landmark immigration legislation would not have passed Congress and been signed into law. Between 1965 and 2015, new immigrants and their offspring accounted for 55 percent of U.S. population growth, according to the Pew Research Center. In the next fifty years, immigrants and their offspring are expected to comprise 88 percent of our country's total population growth. In other words, a country that's been long characterized by its black-and-white binary now faces a far more complex and unparalleled demographic reality.

Wherever I go, I carry a copy of President John F. Kennedy's *A Nation of Immigrants,* a curious book that Kennedy started writing during the 1950s, a curious time in American history. This was the postwar era of Elvis Presley and Marilyn Monroe, when black Americans were denied their civil rights and immigration to the country was restricted by what Kennedy described as "discriminatory national-racial quotas." This is the period that Trump, while campaigning for president under the slogan "Make America Great Again," yearned for. "That's when we had a country. That's when we had borders. Without borders you don't have a country," Trump said of the 1950s, just a few decades after his grandfather emigrated from Germany.

In the book, Kennedy, the grandson of Irish immigrants, argues for welcoming more immigrants to America as he outlines our country's immigration history. "All told," Kennedy writes, "more than 42 million immigrants have come to our shores since the beginning of our history as a nation." The first time I read the book, I was blown away by that number. After doing some research, I learned that because of a 1965 immigration law that Kennedy and his brothers, Robert and Ted, championed, more than forty-three million immigrants have moved to America since, including my grandparents and many aunts, uncles, and cousins. Let that sink in: forty-two million immigrants in 187 years, then forty-three million immigrants in fifty years. That's a lot of change in a perpetually changing America forever resistant to change. It's no wonder that we are where we are.

And for the most part, we are nowhere.

News organizations, by and large, lack the clarity to look at race, immigration, and identity as intersecting issues that affect all Americans from all racial, ethnic, and class backgrounds. Too often, many of my fellow journalists—particularly white journalists, since most newsrooms are led and populated by white people—choose not to call racism what it is, allowing a white supremacist ideology to hide behind phrases like "chain migration," "anchor babies," and "rule of law." All the while, our country's framer-in-chief is President Donald Trump, who considers members of the news media who call out his half-truths and bald-faced lies as "the enemy of the people." If Trump could spark his political career by questioning the citizenship of a sitting American president, who happened to be the country's first African American commander-in-chief, then of course he would question anyone's citizenship. When it comes to immigration and the question of who is welcome here, Trump is the culmination of a festering bipartisan mess and a numbingly complicit public.

When will we connect the dots?

When will we fully face what's in front of us?

Who gets to exercise their rights as U.S. citizens, and why?

While I was filming a documentary at the Pine Ridge Indian Reservation in South Dakota, a student at Crazy Horse School approached me. "I know who you are," the sixteen-year-old said. "You can't talk about immigration and not talk about us." At Pine Ridge, 75 percent of children live below the poverty line. The dropout rate is over 70 percent. Unemployment is between 85 and 90 percent. I'm embarrassed to say that I'd never visited a reservation before; the despair and hopelessness was staggering to witness.

After I spoke in Wilmington, North Carolina, an elderly black woman grabbed me. "I'm not an immigrant, Mr. Vargas," she said. "Our people were brought here against our will." Then she pulled a piece of paper out of her purse and, in a thick southern drawl, continued, "Mr. Vargas, my great-great-grandmother landed near Charleston, South Carolina, and was given this." She opened the yellowed and crumpled paper. It was a bill of sale. I'd never seen one before. "Can you connect the paper she got to the papers that you and your people can't seem to get?"

According to a study by Harvard University, Hurricane Maria, the worst catastrophe in Puerto Rico's history, claimed 4,645 people—killing more people than 9/11 and Hurricane Katrina combined. A few weeks after the tragedy hit, a young man from San Juan emailed me. "Hey Jose," he wrote, "I know you're not a U.S. citizen but are you sure you want to be one? I'm a citizen and it don't guarantee everything, man."

Between 1898 and 1935, the Philippines and Puerto Rico were considered "overseas possessions" by the U.S. government. Though it comes as a shock to some Americans, America still owns Puerto Rico.

18.
Who Am I?

"Who is Jose Antonio Vargas?" read the headline of a column by Jack Shafer.

Then a media critic for Slate, Shafer proceeded to compare me to Janet Cooke, a *Washington Post* reporter who won a Pulitzer in 1981 for an article about an eight-year-old heroin addict whom she had made up. "I know the two lies aren't exactly analogous. Cooke told her lies to inflate her status, Vargas to normalize his," Shafer wrote. "The trouble with habitual liars, and Vargas confesses to having told lie after lie to protect himself from deportation, is that they tend to get too good at it. Lying becomes reflex. And a confessed liar is not somebody you want working on your newspaper. . . .

"There's something about this guy," Shafer concluded, "to make a journalist's nose itch."

I understand Shafer's itchy nose. I cannot stand on a moral high ground, because I lied—repeatedly and knowingly. But his words made me wonder what a journalist is obliged to reveal about his or her life. What privacy do we have a right to regarding our own stories? Had Shafer ever held anything back from his readers, particularly about his personal life? What would have happened if he discovered as a sixteen-year-old that he was an unlawful person in a country that he believed had adopted him as its own? Would he have gone to the nearest airport and flown back to where he had been sent from? What sort of life-altering decisions was he confronted with as a teenager? How did he address them? Journalism is a fishbowl, especially in Washington, D.C. Usually, reporters and editors have less than three degrees of separation. I wanted to email Shafer; he and I had corresponded in the past, after I complimented him on a particular column. I admire his work, and I wanted to talk to him on the phone and explain why I did what I did. But I stopped myself, realizing that I had bigger things to worry about than Jack Shafer's nose.

Journalism mentors of mine, especially those who were journalists of color, urged me to "toughen up." Advocacy and journalism are seen as mutually exclusive, especially if you're a journalist who happens to be a woman, queer, or a person of color, and your mere identity, your very presence, visible or invisible, can be interpreted as political in newsrooms usually run by and populated with straight white men, the framers and enablers of the master narrative. When I first started working in newsrooms in the late 1990s and early and mid-2000s, I was advised not to be so open about being gay. After writing a series of stories about AIDS in Washington, an older editor I admired stopped by my desk one afternoon. "Do you really want to be the gay reporter who writes about AIDS?" said the editor, a white, straight male. "That's not a way to get ahead here at the *Post*." Many journalists, including my own friends, balk at being labeled "advocacy journalists," as if the designation denigrates their work. "Journalists are gonna call you different names—'advocacy journalist,' 'activist journalist,' whatever. What they call you usually reflects how they see themselves," said Marcia Davis, who edited me for years at the *Post*. She's black. "The only thing you can control," Marcia reminded me, "is your work."

But what is my "work"?

Because I had spent thirteen years of my life working in newsrooms, because a journalist was all I'd ever been, I felt disoriented and completely out of my element. I used to have one role: report the hell out of a story, and write it to the best of my ability. Now I had several roles, most of them projected onto me: "*the* face of undocumented immigrants," as if an issue as complex and as charged as illegal immigration can be represented by one face and one story; "a spokesperson for immigrant rights," as if I'm a walking compilation of talking points; and, most perplexing, "an immigrant rights leader." I would never call myself a "leader" and usually run away from people who refer to themselves as such. Suddenly, I was not a human being. By creating Define American with my friends, I claimed an issue and was treated like one.

Here in the U.S., the language we use to discuss immigration does not recognize the realities of our lives based on conditions that we did not create and cannot control. For the most part, why are white people called "expats" while people of color are called "immigrants"? What's the difference between a "settler" and a "refugee"? Language itself is a barrier to information, a fortress against understanding the inalienable instinct of human beings to move. The United States, after all, was founded on this very freedom. A careful reading of the Declaration of Independence makes plain that among the grievances prompting the rebellion against Great Britain was the kingdom's mishandling of migration. Of the declaration's twenty-seven grievances against the monarch, the seventh stated: "He," meaning King George III, "has endeavored to prevent the population of these States; for that purpose obstructing the Laws for Naturalization of Foreigners; refusing to pass others to encourage their migration hither."

A country has a right to define and defend its borders— I understand that reality. But our history, past and present, proves that America has been defining and defending its borders while expanding its reach on its own terms. I also understand that a country has a right to know who resides within its borders and where people come from. That was among the reasons why I outed myself as undocumented. All of that aside, this country of countries, founded on the freedom of movement, must look itself in the mirror, clearly and carefully, before determining the price and cost of who gets to be an American in a globalized and interconnected twenty-first century. This is a twenty-first-century reality that the American government, along with multinational American corporations, has largely sculpted and created, from the wars we start to the iPhones we sell to the television shows and movies we make. This is a twenty-first-century reality in which tweets and Facebook messages travel much faster and more easily than human beings.

Migration is the most natural thing people do, the root of how civilizations, nation-states, and countries were established. The difference, however, is that when white people move, then and now, it's seen as courageous and necessary, celebrated in history books. Yet when people of color move, legally or illegally, the migration itself is subjected to question of legality. Is it a crime? Will they assimilate? When will they stop? There are an estimated 258 million migrants around the world, and many of us are migrating to countries that previously colonized and imperialized us. We have a human right to move, and governments should serve that right, not limit it. The unprecedented movement of people—what some call a "global migration crisis"—is, in reality, a natural progression of history. Yes, we are here because we believe in the promise of the American Dream—the search for a better life, the challenge of dreaming big. But we are also here because you were there—the cost of American imperialism and globalization, the impact of economic policies and political decisions. During this volatile time in the U.S. and around the world, we need a new language around migration and the meaning of citizenship. Our survival depends on the creation and understanding of this new language.

A few months after my coming-out essay was published, I was getting antsy. I didn't understand why I hadn't heard a peep from the government. Moreover, as I started traveling like a walking controversy, I fielded the same questions over and over again about being undocumented, from both journalists and everyday people.

I approached Richard Stengel, then the managing editor of *Time* magazine, about doing a follow-up story. I wanted to write about why I hadn't gotten deported. He introduced me to Tom Weber, an experienced editor who came up with the reportorial structure of what ended up being a five-thousand-word cover story. In the piece, I wrote about the contradic-

142 Jose Antonio Vargas

tions of our immigration debate. Polls showed substantial support for creating a path to citizenship for people like me, yet 52 percent of Americans supported allowing police to stop and question anyone they suspected of being "illegal." Democrats are viewed as being more welcoming to immigrants, but the Obama administration had sharply ramped up deportations. The pro-business Republican Party is home to the most virulent anti-immigrant officials, even though many industries, from agriculture to construction to food processing, depend on cheap labor.

In the piece, I answered questions such as:

Why don't you become legal?

Why did you get your driver's license when you knew it wasn't legal?

So you're not Mexican?

Why did you come out?

For the final question, I spoke to Gaby, the young undocumented Ecuadoran whom I had met and befriended. Gaby moved to the U.S. in 1993, the same year I did. Immigration officials raided her home in 2006; her family was rounded up, and her father had to wear an ankle bracelet. She's been fighting against their deportation since. Gaby, who has three education degrees, wants to be a special education teacher. But her life remains on hold as she watches documented friends land jobs and plan their futures.

"For many people, coming out is a way of saying you're not alone," Gaby told me. "In our movement, you come out for yourself, and you come out for other people."

Originally, *Time* editors wanted to put me on the cover. As I didn't want Define American to be the Jose Antonio Vargas show, I proposed an alternative: "What if I got thirty or so undocumented young people to agree to be on the cover?" I asked Paul Moakley, one of the photo editors.

Paul looked surprised.

"How are you going to find them? Are they going to be willing to be photographed? Can we use their names?"

I asked Paul to give me a couple of days to figure it out. When I hung up with Paul, I called Gaby. Immediately, we came up with a plan. I started calling Dreamers I knew: Cesar Vargas in New York, Erika Andiola in Arizona, Julio Salgado and Mandeep Chahal in California, this kid named Victor that I had just met during my trip to Alabama. Gaby, for her part, knew way more people than I did. She was particularly excited to invite Lorella Praeli, a young undocumented Peruvian from Connecticut. I was adamant that the cover photo needed to be representative of the entire undocumented population, so we needed to find undocumented Asians, blacks, and white immigrants, too. Thankfully, Tony Choi, who was born in South Korea, Tolu Olubunmi, who was born in Nigeria, and Manuel Bartsch, who was born in Germany, all agreed to participate.

At this point, Define American was an all-volunteer organization that had no money. I had no money. If I asked *Time* to cover flights and hotel rooms for undocumented people, some of whom had never flown before, I was afraid editors might get antsy and back out. So I asked Frank Sharry, a longtime advocate, a walking history book of immigration policies, if America's Voice, his organization, could cover it. Not only did he say yes, he connected me with his colleague Pili Tobar, who offered to help out with logistics. Lucia Allain, a young undocumented Peruvian, was especially helpful in coordinating schedules. I was most worried about Victor, who was flying from Birmingham. He had never been on an airplane, never gone through an airport. To get through security, he planned to use his Mexican passport, the only government-issued ID he had. Many undocumented people use passports from their countries of origin to get on domestic flights. I had to do the same. As my lawyers had feared, the Washington State Department of Licensing canceled my license two weeks after I disclosed my undocumented status. One of my lawyers suggested I get a valid passport from the Philippine Embassy, which I did. These passports don't have visas, which can trigger TSA agents to check their immigration status. It's risky, especially so if your passport is from Mexico, given how often people of Mexican descent are racially profiled. We wanted to make sure Victor had all the information to make a decision for himself. We coached him on how to get through TSA: don't look nervous, make sure your hands are not shaking when you show your passport, don't smile too much. To our relief, he made it through the airport.

Within forty-eight hours, we had assembled thirty-five Dreamers in a warehouse studio in the Meatpacking District for a photo shoot. Most of them didn't know each other. Everyone gave their permission to appear on a cover of a major magazine—I couldn't tell them which one—and I made sure I didn't make any promises, in case it didn't work out for some reason. Their trust in me, and most of them knew me by name only, was humbling.

The photo shoot, which lasted for several hours, was among the proudest days of my entire life. The photographer,

Gian Paul Lozza, and his assistants treated everyone with such dignity. There were makeup artists to make sure everyone got a touch-up before the group photo and their individual portraits. I thought of Ellen DeGeneres on the cover of *Time* and what that image meant to me. I could only imagine what this cover image—so many faces with names and stories—could mean for other undocumented people.

When the group photo was selected, and when it was confirmed that indeed thirty-five undocumented people would be featured on the cover of *Time,* I sent an email to one of the top editors. I had a request. I told him, whatever you do, please do not call us "illegal" on the cover of *Time.*

The headline of the cover story, which ended up being the cover story for all of *Time*'s international editions, read: "We Are Americans, Just Not Legally."

There were murmurs that the Obama administration was crafting a policy that would temporarily shield undocumented young Americans from deportation and give them work permits and allow them to drive. I had heard something was up, but I wasn't sure. Gaby knew more than I did because she had been lobbying the Obama White House. Sensitive to criticism that he was the "Deporter-in-Chief," Obama and his team had been weighing their options. Part of the equation, I'm sure, was the impending presidential election, where the Latino vote could be a deciding factor.

Whatever the factors were, on June 15, 2012, the day the *Time* cover story hit newsstands, President Obama announced the creation of what would be known as DACA, short for Deferred Action for Childhood Arrivals. Immediately, DACA was deemed "a presidential overreach." In the Fox News–

Drudge–Breitbart universe, it was considered something like "amnesty," which it most certainly is not. At its idealistic core, one can look at DACA as the most significant development in the fight for immigrant rights since President Reagan signed the Immigration Reform and Control Act in 1986. With DACA, nearly 850,000 young undocumented Americans could pursue their dreams. But here's the realistic version: to be enrolled in DACA, you have to pay the government nearly five hundred dollars so it won't deport you for two years from the only country that you've known as your home. DACA is temporary, and not everyone qualifies.

Of the thirty-five Dreamers on the *Time* cover, six couldn't apply for DACA for various reasons. I was one of them. The age cutoff was thirty years old, and I was a little over four months too old. I was disappointed. My family, especially Lola, was more disappointed than I was. I don't know the toll that my public life and its concomitant threats and criticisms have taken on Lola. I remember her calling me the day after DACA was announced, when she realized that I wasn't included.

"Okay ka lang pa, apo ko?" ("Are you doing okay, grandson?")

Yes.

"Alam ko ang dami mong sinakripisyo." ("I know you've sacrificed a lot.")

Not as much as you have, I said.

I could hear Lola crying on the phone.

About a week after the *Time* cover hit newsstands, I was in the security line at John F. Kennedy International Airport. The TSA agent, a twenty-something black woman in a ponytail, gave me a little nod, like she knew who I was. I felt my arms tighten. I grabbed my phone, just in case I needed to call someone right away. When it was my turn to show her my Philippine passport—now the only piece of ID I had to travel—with no visa in it, I was prepared for whatever could happen.

She smiled when I handed her my passport.

"You're Jose, right?" she asked, lowering her voice so no one could hear. "My brother-in-law is undocumented. I actually bought the magazine." She pulled out the *Time* magazine from her bag and asked me to sign it.

19.
Inside Fox News

"I should have called ICE," Tucker Carlson told me seconds before his show went live on Fox News. It was May 2017. I don't know how serious he was about calling ICE, but the fact that he would even consider such a stunt reminded me how hard it is for some Americans to regard undocumented people three-dimensionally. Tucker was fiddling with his tie as I sat across from him inside his studio in Washington, D.C. Underneath all that bravado is a fidgety guy.

He added: "That would have been good TV."

That's what I was there for: "good TV." The fact that it angered me, made me uncomfortable, and threw off my center—all that was irrelevant. In fact, the agitated, nervous energy that took hold in my entire body made me even better for TV. Carlson knew that, and I imagine that's why he said what he said. Worse, I knew it, too, but couldn't control my nerves.

It's difficult to overstate the role the Fox News Channel has played in framing, disseminating, and cementing the anti-immigrant narrative that was central in electing Trump. No other news channel, I would argue, has dominated a single issue the way Fox News has molded immigration. Though not everyone watches Fox, it's been the most-watched cable news channel for more than twelve years, shaping the perception of immigrants and our families, especially for people who have no direct interaction with us and know us only through the media they consume. Anti-immigrant organizations with ties to white nationalism (the Federation for American Immigration Reform, the Center for Immigration Studies, and Numbers USA, among them) have gone from being considered fringe groups to being viewed as credible sources because of their ubiquity on Fox. News outlets like NPR, the *New York Times,* and the *Washington Post* rely on the leaders of these groups for their "expertise" so that they can claim "balance" in their reporting. These well-funded, well-organized, anti-immigrant groups command the right on a level unmatched by progressives on the left who struggle to come up with a unifying and accessible message.

On Fox, "illegals" are cast as enemies, a collective "burden" to society, "draining" public programs and "stealing" jobs from native-born Americans. We are the criminalized and criminal Other, thoroughly un-American and unwilling to become American. Though Fox News did not create Trump, it gave him an issue to own and a kingdom to reign over.

At first I was conflicted about appearing on Fox. I didn't want to be just another character in their script, complicit in their theatricality. I did not want to be used. But my friend Jehmu Greene, a cofounder of Define American, changed my mind. An unabashed progressive, Jehmu is a paid contributor on Fox News. She's one of the very few black female voices on the network. "Look, it's either you're on Fox dismantling stereotypes about immigration in front of viewers who may call you illegal to your face," Jehmu said, "or, you can just speak to the choir."

I've appeared on Fox News numerous times in the past few years, mostly interviewed by Carlson, Bill O'Reilly, Megyn Kelly, and Lou Dobbs. Every hit on Fox requires careful preparation, which always boils down to making sure I am sufficiently calm before getting in front of the camera. And keeping my cool translates to controlling my thick and bushy eyebrows, which are the most expressive and most uncontrollable part of my face. The Fox producers who have booked me have been very kind and exceedingly polite, as if they know how much energy it takes for me to appear on their shows.

Still, there was no preparing me for that moment when O'Reilly, in November 2014, told me on-air: "You and the other people here illegally don't deserve to be here. That's harsh, it's harsh, okay?"

Was I supposed to respond with "okay"? It was only my second time on O'Reilly's show; the first had been a satellite interview. O'Reilly is like everyone's cranky uncle, as brash and boorish in person as he is on-air.

Our interview was on the same day President Obama announced that he was expanding DACA, which would protect more immigrants, including older Dreamers like me and undocumented parents of children who are U.S. citizens. I was caught off guard by what O'Reilly said. All I could do was repeat it inside my head—except I actually verbalized what I was thinking.

"I don't deserve—" I said on-air.

O'Reilly, as he is wont to do, interrupted. "Okay? You don't have an entitlement to be here."

I corrected him.

"I don't feel entitled to be here," I said. I tried hard not raise an eyebrow, not to seem visibly angry or upset. "This is where I grew up, this is my home, my family is here."

For weeks the exchange clouded and corrupted my mind. The only thought that cleared it was when I finally said to myself: What has O'Reilly done to "deserve" to be here? I only wish I could have thought of that question and asked him on-air.

I was even more unprepared two years later, when producers added a last-minute guest to the lineup of an interview I was scheduled to do during the Republican National Convention in Cleveland. Originally, the interview was supposed to be between Kelly and me. But before I went on-air, I was told that another guest was added: Laura Wilkerson, whose son, Josh, was killed by an undocumented immigrant. Producers sat us next to each other during the live hit.

"Let me start with you, Laura," said Kelly as I sat uncomfortably in my chair, knitting my eyebrows. As a group of people, Kelly calls us "illegals" or "illegal immigrants." In person, to my face, she always refers to me as undocumented.

"You want a harder stance on illegal immigration," Kelly continued. "And you're sitting next to Jose, who is himself an admitted undocumented immigrant. I mean, is it hard to look at him and say, 'I want you kicked out'? You know, 'I want the Trump plan that would lead to you being removed'?"

My stomach dropped. I could feel myself shrinking. I wanted to walk out of the interview. To this day, I don't know how I managed to stay seated.

"I think if you're not a United States citizen, you don't

have a seat at the table regardless, especially where you're making laws," Wilkerson responded. I could feel her vitriol, wrapped in such profound loss. "You just don't have a seat at the table."

But I was seated right next to her. We were sharing a table.

At the moment, the only thing I could do was turn toward her and acknowledge her pain.

"I'm really sorry about [your loss]," I said. "We're at the mercy of congresspeople, Congress members who haven't done anything."

"It's not up to Congress to do something," Wilkerson said. "It's up to you to get in line and become an American citizen."

She continued.

"There is a law. It needs to be enforced. Close the borders. Enforce current laws and, you know, welcome to America if you come in the front door."

"Actually, ma'am, there is no line for me to get in the back of," I said to her. I told myself: Look her in the eye. Don't cut her off. Be polite. I continued: "That's why we need for something to happen. I'll be here twenty-three years next month—"

"Then you've had plenty of time," Wilkerson said.

"If there was a process, I would have done it."

Kelly interjected and told Wilkerson that I was brought to America. A few seconds that seemed like hours passed before Kelly asked Wilkerson if she favored any sort of path to legalization for immigrants like me.

"Get in line, and come in and tell us who you are," Wilkerson said. "We have a right to know who's in this country. So that's the only thing I believe. You know, they've put themselves in harm by coming here."

There was no time to respond to what Wilkerson said.

I wanted to keep repeating: there is no line.

I wanted to scream, over and over again: THERE IS NO LINE! THERE IS NO LINE! THERE IS NO LINE!

I wanted to tell her that when it comes to harm, she has no idea, just like I have no idea what it's like to lose a son. Indescribable, the harm, all around.

20.
Public Person, Private Self

I've never considered myself an activist. In fact, I wasn't sure I knew the word's exact definition, so I looked it up. According to Merriam-Webster, "activist" is both a noun and an adjective. An "activist" is "a person who uses or supports strong actions (such as public protests) in support of or opposition to one side of a controversial issue." Whatever the definition, and leaving aside what I support or oppose, my public declaration of being undocumented was considered a form of activism by people from the left and the right.

Since I am visible on social media, the attacks and demands from all sorts of people—from the left and the right, from people of all backgrounds—run deep.

On any given day, people who've seen me on Fox News or read about me on conservative sites like Breitbart News, the *Daily Caller,* and Newsmax send private and public messages demanding my arrest and deportation. In the first days and weeks of the Trump presidency, tweets like "Christmas came early this year. It will be even earlier next year when @joseiswriting becomes Deportee #1" and "Hope your bags are packed @joseiswriting" started flooding my Twitter feed.

Once news reports started circulating that officers from Immigration and Customs Enforcement are targeting "high-profile illegal immigrants," a slew of messages landed on my feed, most from users who don't use their real names or real photos on their profiles. Usually, I ignore them. But this tweet from John Cardillo, host of a daily show, *America Talks Live,* on Newsmax, and whose account is verified by Twitter, was hard to ignore:

Hey @joseiswriting,

Tick tock

"ICE Detains Illegal Immigrant Activists."

Often, I ignore the tweets, Facebook messages, and emails. To deal with how personal people online can get, how cutting and revolting their language is, I've thought of myself as the subject of a news story. I try, as hard as I can, to look at the hateful words and the deplorable phrases with distance and detachment. They're not talking about me. They don't even know me. This "illegal alien" person they're describing with such vulgarity is someone else. It's not me.

Not all the reaction, online and off, is negative. After my first appearance on *The O'Reilly Factor* in June 2012, I received an email from Dennis Murphy of Omaha, Nebraska, who described himself as the founder and former state chairman of the Nebraska Minutemen, which had merged with the Nebraska Tea Party. "I was positively impressed by your interview with Bill O'Reilly," Murphy wrote. "You now refer to yourself in your blog as 'an undocumented American,' which I believe is a fair and accurate assessment."

And sometimes the people who follow me on Twitter and

watch me on Fox News are not at all who I think they are, in the same way that I'm not who they think I am.

"Is it you? Are you the 'illegal' guy on Fox?" said the tall, middle-aged white man in khakis and a striped white shirt and oversize black coat. He and I were standing in the Delta Air Lines terminal at Tampa International Airport, waiting to board a flight to LaGuardia Airport. It was February 2015. I had just given a speech at the Black, Brown & College Bound Summit for African American and Latino students at a hotel in downtown Tampa. I was headed to New York City for meetings.

Sometimes, because of TV appearances, I get recognized in public, mostly at airports and Starbucks. It's been about 70–30: most people are supportive, and many of them "come out" to me as undocumented. Some get a little aggressive, asking why I have still not gotten deported. More often than not, I engage in conversations. But I was too tired to engage that afternoon in Tampa. Instead of answering, I half-nodded, then walked away, lugging my carry-on bag.

I've spent more time in airports and planes than in whatever apartment I was living at. I changed apartments four times in the past seven years (New York City, Washington, D.C., San Francisco, Los Angeles), as I traveled to countless cities and towns in forty-eight states, doing more than a thousand events: speaking at panels, giving speeches, visiting schools, meeting with all kinds of people from all backgrounds. I fly so much, especially on Delta Air Lines and American Airlines, that I often get upgraded to first class, as I was that afternoon.

A few seconds after I boarded the plane, as I was stowing my luggage, the white man in the oversize black coat grabbed my left shoulder as he walked by. "I didn't know illegals fly first class," he said.

I sat down. I wasn't sure if anyone else heard him, but the woman clutching her iPad across the aisle must have seen my face. I was upset. I'd been used to all the words, but that was the first time I had been touched, and I didn't know how to react. I felt violated. I was mad. I put on my headset and tried to get lost in my thoughts with Ella Fitzgerald and Joni Mitchell. That didn't work. A few minutes later, after the flight had taken off, I stood up and headed to the bathroom, even though I did not need to go to the bathroom. I wanted to see where he was sitting, which was near the middle of the plane, in a middle seat between two women. He didn't see me looking at him. At least I don't think he did.

What was his story? Why did he think it was okay to grab me like that? Did it make him feel good? Feel better, stronger? Superior? What was going through his mind when he decided that his hand should land on my shoulder? What else did he want to say? What else did he want to do?

And what should I do?

I bought Wi-Fi access and got on my personal Facebook page, which only my friends and relatives can see. I summarized what happened and ended the post with: "This is gonna be an awkward flight."

"Awkward for whom?" wrote my friend Tricia. "You're the one flying in style while he gets coach. As it should be."

I wish I could listen to my friend Glenn, who wrote: "You

upset him, just by being yourself and doing the right thing. You win! Don't give him one more thought or one more second of your time."

This wasn't about winning or losing, and I couldn't stop thinking about him in that middle seat. I'm a big guy and his shoulders were bigger than mine. Not fun for the middle seat.

Todd chimed in: "Ask the flight attendant to send back some champagne to him and watch his head explode."

Should I tell the flight attendant?

I didn't know what to do until I read what Graciela wrote: "So you're in First Class and he's not? Sounds perfect."

After reading that comment, I decided to talk to the guy.

Once we landed at LaGuardia International Airport, I grabbed my bags and waited for him to get out of the plane. He was surprised to see me waiting outside the terminal.

"I'm Jose," I said.

"Eric." I asked if it was Eric with a *c* or Eric with a *k*, and it was the former. He wouldn't give me his last name.

I told him that I got upgraded to first class because I travel so much. The upgrade, I said, was free.

"Must be nice," Eric said.

"Yes, it is," I said, feeling upset at myself for wanting to explain myself. I don't owe this guy an explanation. Why am I talking to him?

"Look, I didn't mean to seem like a jerk. I've seen you on TV. Bragging."

"Bragging about what?"

"Being illegal."

I told him that it wasn't something I brag about. It's not

something I'm proud of. It's something I want to fix, and that there's no way to fix it.

"You want to get legal?"

"Of course. Why would I want to be like this?"

"Oh."

He lives in New Jersey, right outside of Trenton. He said he was forty-eight, and he had just gotten laid off from his job at an insurance company, where he had worked for almost a decade. He's divorced with two kids, both teenagers. After about fifteen minutes of conversation, as we made our way into the baggage claim area, he felt the need to point out that he voted for Obama twice. I told him Obama had deported more immigrants than any other modern president, a fact that seemed to surprise him.

"Politics," he said, shrugging.

"Fucking politics," I said.

I gave him my business card and wrote DefineAmeri can.com/facts on the back of it. That site, I told him, has all the facts he would ever need to know about immigration. I wanted to ask him if he knew where his ancestors came from, if he knew what papers they had when they moved to America. But I didn't. I told him I needed to go, and we parted ways. I've yet to hear from him on email.

It's not only people who've seen me on Fox News who appoint themselves as immigration officials questioning why I'm here.

In May 2018, I was invited to speak at a symposium on early life stress. Organized and hosted by the Picower Institute for Learning and Memory at the Massachusetts Institute of Technology, the gathering attracted a who's who of experts on children's mental health. Barbara Picower, an early booster and supporter of Define American, kicked off the daylong conference and sat in the front row. I'd never been surrounded by so many pediatricians, researchers, and scientists, all grappling with how to study and combat what everybody was calling "toxic stress." The first speaker was Dr. Nadine Burke Harris, the founder of the Center for Youth Wellness, whose TED talk, "How Childhood Trauma Affects Health Across a Lifetime," has more than 3.7 million views. Before Geoffrey Canada, the creator of the much-lauded Harlem Children's Zone, took the podium to close out the day, I participated in a panel. About a hundred people were in the room. Some people had either seen me on TV or heard my story. Some people had not. After my brief talk, a middle-aged woman sitting in the middle of the room raised her hand. She looked like she was South Asian.

"I find your comments very offensive, because we are immigrants, we came legally to this country, we followed all the rules," she said, looking me straight in the eye.

I could feel the room's temperature heighten.

The woman continued.

"You should not group together legal and illegal immigrants because we followed every rule that the U.S. told us to follow. We didn't break any laws and we entered this country legally."

A young woman was seated directly in front of the older South Asian woman. She looked increasingly uncomfortable, eventually appearing to melt into her seat. I thought I heard some people gasp. Others looked at me in horror.

The older woman went on, her voice rising.

"You've broken the laws of this country! Don't bind legal with illegal. We are different. We are not you."

At that point, I jumped in. Don't lose your cool, I started telling myself. Don't yell. Don't get mad. Don't lose your cool.

"I hear this a lot, and it's really important that we address it. Out of thirty-four people in my Filipino American family, I'm the only one who's undocumented. So you cannot separate the 'legal' from the 'illegal,'" I said. "And, by the way, I am here illegally, but as a human being, I cannot be illegal because that doesn't exist. People cannot be illegal."

She cut me off.

"You had a chance to become legal because of amnesty."

"Which was in 1986," I interjected. "I came here in 1993."

One of the symposium's organizers intervened and said the conversation was off topic. I wanted to keep going. I wanted to show everyone in the room that when it comes to immigration, the ignorance and indifference go far beyond the confines of Fox News, conservative radio, and Breitbart. They were right here at MIT.

After the panel, the attendees started spilling out of the room. I looked for the woman and found her. She wouldn't give me her name. She said she emigrated from India and that she became a U.S. citizen because of her husband. She also told me that she was an immigration lawyer. I was floored. If an immigration lawyer was foggy on the history of America's immigration policies, then who could be expected to keep it straight? She was condemning me for not following a process that didn't exist. Breathe, I told myself. Breathe in. Breathe out. Find compassion for this woman.

"All the resources that are going to the illegals should be going to the blacks," she said, referring to Canada's speech. Canada is African American. "They're Americans. You're not."

I gave her my business card and walked away.

21.
Progress

I'm neither a Republican nor a Democrat. I don't identify as a liberal or a conservative. In my mind, progress—being progressive—should not be limited by politics, and certainly not dictated by one party. But since I'm an undocumented and gay person of color, I'm considered a progressive. And the thing about being an "activist" in progressive circles is, you're never enough.

As difficult as it's been to be exposed to the blatant ignorance and naked hatred of people from the right, it's been equally emotionally taxing to be subjected to the unrealistic expectations and demands of the left. Identifying people as "right" or "left" is a risky overgeneralization, of course. But as someone who gets attacked by both sides, for various reasons, I'll take the risk.

I'm a relative newcomer to the immigrant rights movement, which, depending on who is telling the story, has been around for decades, replenished and recharged in the mid-2000s by young undocumented people coming of age in the era of text messaging and social media. Essentially, there are two movements separated by geography and money. There is the movement in Washington, D.C., largely led by immigration-centric groups, many of them Latinos (and some Asians) who are directly impacted by the issue. They are mostly aligned with Democrats and progressives, and in recent years, business leaders like Michael Bloomberg, Rupert Murdoch (yes, the same Murdoch who owns Fox News), and Mark Zuckerberg have joined the fray. (Mark got involved when he found out that a student he was mentoring was undocumented.) Then there's the movement in other cities and states, which too often take a backseat to the backroom partisan deals of the headline-grabbing Washington scene. I wasn't really aware of the generational, geographic, and financial dynamic when I outed myself as undocumented and started Define American. I valued my independence, which was threatening to some people who wondered why I was bothering to go on Fox News and why I was willing to engage Republicans.

From the outset, I made it clear that I was neither an activist nor an organizer. I report, I write, I make documentaries. Before I publicly declared my undocumented status, I started producing a documentary to capture, in real time, the journey I was on and document the people I meet. I called the film *Documented*. Nevertheless, to some longtime activists and organizers, my arrival to their movement was "too late" and my story was "too complicated." Some professional advocates didn't know what to do with me. When Jake, a cofounder of Define American, approached the Partnership for a New American Economy, a pro-immigrant group started by a coalition of business leaders like Bloomberg and Murdoch, for a possible collaboration, he was rebuffed. Jake told me: "The guy I met with said, 'We admire Jose, but he admitted to committing fraud to get jobs, and we can't really be seen as promoting that.'" So much for telling the truth. I thought to myself, do the people who run this group know actual undocumented people and understand what we have to do to survive?

Weeks after the *Times* published my coming-out story in 2011, I had lunch with a seasoned immigrant rights organizer in D.C. He was the first one to voice what other veteran foot soldiers had been saying, which was something along the lines of: while people were protesting on the streets in 2006—when hundreds of thousands of immigrants, documented and undocumented, flooded the country's biggest cities, including D.C.—I was working at the *Washington Post*, hiding my secret, building my career. "You can't blame people for asking, 'Is this a career move, too?' This instant celebrity?"

The criticism caught me off guard. From my point of view, I sacrificed my entire professional life for my personal freedom. I knew that declaring my undocumented status would elevate my public profile—that comes with the territory—but celebrity was and never is the goal. If this were any kind of "career move," it was, I thought, a detour—my journalistic and documentary filmmaking career could have gone in multiple directions. As immigration lawyers had warned me months before, revealing my undocumented status in such a highly visible way would render me unemployable. I had to worry about making money to support myself and my family, since Mama and my siblings in the Philippines depended on a monthly allowance that I'd been providing for years. My sister Czarina, who was attending her last year of college, was especially worried. *"Kuya,"* she asked me on the phone, *"pwede pa rin ba akong makatapos ng kolehiyo?"* ("Older brother, can I still finish college?") Though I'd saved up some money that I could live on for a few months, it ran out sooner than I had planned for. By March 2012, nine months after my public disclosure, I had $250.84 left in my checking account and $66.74 in savings. If Jake, Alicia, and Jehmu had not lent me some money, I would not have made it. Jake transferred money to my Bank of America account so I could make rent. It took a few more months to come up with a creative *and* legal solution. Forming my own organization would allow me to apply my skills to help rewrite the master narrative of immigration. And because I was no longer employable, being an undocumented entrepreneur would allow me to work within the confines of the law.

A few longtime activists viewed me with suspicion that sometimes bordered on benign but palpable rejection. I was deemed "too privileged," "an opportunist," "elite." "You're too successful to represent us," an undocumented day laborer told me at a rally in November 2013, turning away before he could hear me say that I had no intention of representing anyone but myself. I did hear him say, under his breath, "You're not even Mexican." The day laborer, a man in his fifties, was buying into the master narrative of who undocumented immigrants are supposed to be and what we're supposed to do.

His comment cut deeper than anything any troll online has ever said to me, haunting me for days. I struggled to understand the root of his frustration. Was he insulted that I passed? Was he assuming that I wanted to live some version of the "good immigrant"/"model minority" trope? Was he frustrated that someone who is not Mexican, an ethnic identity that's become synonymous with immigration, was taking too much space? Am I taking too much space? How much space should I take? Do I feel guilty that I managed to pass because of the color of my skin or a Tagalog accent I suppressed? What kind of test must I pass now?

Younger activists weren't quite sure what to make of me. While they had spent their high school and college years fighting for the DREAM Act, organizing online and on the streets, I was working in newsrooms, lying about my immigration status and passing as a U.S. citizen so I could get well-paying jobs. An activist wrote me in an email that she was unhappy that I revealed so many details about being undocumented, including getting a driver's license. "I thought to myself that it was very selfish of you to [write] that," she said, "because this could potentially hurt our community and people like my father who has had to pay for getting a driver's license for the past 10 years."

She continued: "When I read about you, I thought, 'We've been fighting for so long. Where has this guy been?'" I was too busy lying and passing. Now I was trying to make up for lost time.

The interrogation of my motives and strategies continued for years, to the point that, as a proactive measure, I started referring to myself as "the most privileged undocumented immigrant in America." It was one way of erecting armor against the criticism. It was also a way of putting up another mask. I exchanged a life of passing as an American and a U.S. citizen so I could work for a life of constantly claiming my privilege so I could exist in the progressive activist world.

The task of dismantling the mass detention and deportation of immigrants is so towering that people who are supposedly on the same side try to stand taller than the next person. Internecine fighting has plagued all kinds of movements since time immemorial. The difference now, however, is the publicness of social media. It's not enough we attack systems, we also battle each other, out in the open. Bullying is commonplace. In the past few years of navigating the progressive activist circle, I've learned that there are all kinds of borders, none higher, steeper, more consequential than the borders between human beings—even among people who are fighting for the same thing but may not even agree on how to define what that thing is.

Since I was mentored and nurtured by both white people and black people, my instinct is to bring people together. In the same way that Mrs. Denny didn't want to leave me behind, I don't want to leave anyone behind, either. That may seem Messianic, perhaps a tad Pollyannaish, but that's how I've been built. We must combat anti-blackness in all communities, especially in non-black immigrant communities. Anti-black racism among Latinos, Asians, Arabs, and Middle Easterners is the other side of the white supremacy coin. We must fight white supremacy wherever it exists, within both progressive and conservative circles.

A month after Trump announced he was running for president, MTV aired, as part of its Look Different campaign, an hourlong primetime special called *White People*. MTV collaborated with Define American on the film, which was produced by Punched Productions, overseen by the wife-and-husband duo of Amelia Kaplan D'Entrone and Craig D'Entrone. I directed the special, which, in many ways, was the visual continuation of the question I posed back in 2003 in a front page article in the *San Francisco Chronicle*: "What is 'white'?"

Well, based on the interviews we conducted, the answers range from lost, confused, to in denial.

Led by producers Erika Clarke and Shauna Siggelkow, the crew and I filmed for three months, interviewing white Millennials across the country, including Katy, an eighteen-year-old from Arizona who was convinced that being white prevented her from receiving college scholarships, a myth that I was surprised so many white people I interviewed, regardless of political orientation, believed to be true. In fact, white students disproportionately get more scholarships than students of color. MTV conducted a nationally representative survey of Millennials. Some of the results were unexpected. I didn't know that the typical white American lives in a town that is more than three-quarters white. I also didn't realize that the average white person's group of friends is more than 90 percent white. Which means that many white people's interactions with people of color and immigrants are limited to what they consume in media: the news that inform their worldview, the TV shows and movies that comprise their system of reality.

Most shocking to me was finding out that nearly 50 percent of white Americans say that discrimination against whites is as big a problem as discrimination against minorities. And these were the young people. What about their parents? Why do they think what they think? And in my experience, many people of color, including immigrants, can be as isolated from white people as white people are to them. White people are seen less as individuals but as oppressive, overwhelming systems, systems they are ignorant of or indifferent to, if not blindly complicit in. So, where do we all meet?

While barnstorming the country for Define American, I came to the realization that everyone feels excluded from America, even the very people whose ancestors created systems of exclusion and oppression. Then, as I interviewed subjects for the MTV special, I wondered: Now, what? What is our vision for a more inclusive, more equitable America? What does that feel like and look like? Where do white people fit in it? How do we demolish white supremacy without pushing more white people to white nationalism?

After *White People* aired in July 2015, I told anyone who would listen, particularly my friends who were political reporters, that I thought Trump would win. Based on my travels and my experiences, Trump hit a nerve outside of the black-and-white binary, far beyond the bubble the East Coast politicos exist within. They all told me I was nuts. They all apologized after he won.

Four days after Trump's election, I flew to Atlanta to give a keynote speech at Facing Race, a three-day conference presented by Race Forward: The Center for Racial Justice Innovation. It's the yearly gathering of "racial justice" and "social justice" activists and organizers where panels, workshops, and breakout sessions have titles like "Multiracial Movements for Black Lives," which featured Alicia Garza, one of the cofounders of the Black Lives Matter movement, and Michelle Alexander, author of the seminal book *The New Jim Crow*. The vibe of the crowd in the auditorium was edgy and restless, the frustration and confusion all bottled up. Then, fifteen minutes into my planned remarks, which I had rewritten to address what immigrant communities should expect in Trump's America, I was heckled by a young man whom news reports identified as Jonathan Perez, an undocumented immigrant of black, Colombian, and indigenous background. Perez was at the back of the room, and I couldn't fully hear him. I read from news reports afterward that he shouted that U.S. citizenship and American identification "should not be a desirable goal for undocumented people."

What I did hear him yell was: "What if we don't want to be American?" Followed by: "I don't want to be American!"

Publicly, in front of almost two thousand people, I said that I define American by the people who have been excluded from the promise of America, which includes African Americans and Native Americans. I recited a quote from James Baldwin, words that I committed to memory the moment I read them while scouring through books at the Mountain View Public Library: "I love America more than any other country in the world and, exactly for this reason, I insist on the right to criticize her perpetually."

Privately, I was spent. I get what he was saying. American citizenship is not the be-all and end-all for everyone. American citizenship is not as simple as being born in America or pledging allegiance to the American flag during a naturalization ceremony. American citizenship is not a guarantee. Talk to indigenous people and black people; even though they may be U.S. citizens by birth, many are treated like second-class citizens. Talk to undocumented people whose idea of citizenship is providing for their families and feeding their kids. Talk to legal permanent residents—green card holders—who decided not to take the next step of applying for U.S. citizenship. Some can't afford the fee, which is about $725. Others feel that America is not home to them, and they're not made to feel like America is home. America is simply where they live, where they work, where they make money. And for some, home is the culture of their home country, not the culture of an adopted land that asks them to assimilate, whatever that may mean.

I wish I could say that being a global citizen is enough, but I haven't been able to see the world, and I'm still trying to figure out what citizenship, from any country, means to me. I wish I could say that being a human being is enough, but there are times I don't feel like a human being.

I feel like a thing. A thing to be explained and understood, tolerated and accepted. A thing that spends too much time educating people so it doesn't have to educate itself on what it has become. I feel like a thing that can't just be.

PART III
Hiding

1.
My Government, Myself

I am not hiding from my government. My government is hiding from me.

At least that's how it's felt in the past seven years, living a public life as undocumented while practicing what I call "radical transparency," which has taken on various forms. Some people accuse me of pulling "stunts," as if I find some kind of masochistic joy out of living in limbo. Then some people argue that I'm not radical enough, that I don't do enough. In their minds, I should be leading rallies, participating in protests, maybe tying myself to the White House. But the only way I've been able to survive the discomfort and distress of the past seven years is doing what I know how to do, what Mrs. Dewar at Mountain View High School said I was good at: asking questions.

"Are you planning on deporting me?" I asked the immigration officer on the phone.

It was May 2012. I prepared myself for the worst after publicly declaring my undocumented status: possible arrest and detention, at any time of any day. The only thing I didn't prepare for was silence. Especially from the government. Particularly the folks from Immigration and Customs Enforcement (ICE), which had removed nearly four hundred thousand individuals from the country in fiscal year 2011, which ended September 30, 2011—exactly one hundred days after I outed myself in the *New York Times*. In 2010 nearly 393,000 immigrants were deported. A year before that, almost 390,000 people. John Morton, who led ICE, touted the 2011 deportation numbers, calling them the result of "smart and effective immigration enforcement" that depended on "setting clear priorities for removal and executing on those priorities."

"I haven't heard from you," I said to the officer as I introduced myself. I told her I was done hiding. I confessed how anxious I was that I'd heard nothing from ICE, nothing from the Department of Homeland Security, nothing from the Department of Justice.

The officer, who was working at the ICE branch in New York City, where I was living at the time, was confused. She said she knew who I was.

"Why are you calling us?" she said.

"Because I want to know what you want to do with me."

"What are you doing?"

"What are *you* doing?"

The agent placed me on hold.

A few days after the new year in 2013, I heard from the office of Senator Patrick Leahy, who chaired the Senate Judiciary Committee. His office asked me to testify as part of the opening salvo in the latest push to pass immigration reform, a priority for the Obama administration. President Obama, who couldn't have won the White House without the Latino vote in 2008 and 2012, failed in his promise to tackle the issue in his first year in office, when Democrats controlled both the House and the Senate. Since I couldn't wrangle any answers from the immigration officer on the phone, I wanted to take my questions directly to congressional members. After all, two of the country's most anti-immigrant senators, Jeff Sessions and Ted Cruz, sat on the committee. Janet Napolitano, who headed DHS, was also asked to testify. To my mind, nothing says *I am done hiding from my government* more than appearing before Congress. I wanted to make it a family affair. Jake Brewer, one of my best friends, took care of the logistics, flying everyone from California to Washington: Lola, Auntie Aida, and Uncle Conrad, joined by Pat, Rich, and Jim. Jake made sure they were all taken care of. *"Itong si Jake ay sobrang mabait at marespeto,"* Uncle Conrad said upon arriving at his hotel. ("This Jake guy is very, very nice and very polite.")

I don't recall ever being as nervous as I was on the day of the hearing. Writing the testimony, which couldn't be longer than five minutes, was daunting enough. I felt prepared to answer whatever questions they lobbed at me. The source of anxiety came from the terror of losing my composure and breaking down. In front of congressional members. In front of my family. In front of other undocumented immigrants, who started piling into the hearing room.

"I come to you as one of our country's eleven million undocumented immigrants, many of us Americans at heart, but without the right papers to show for it," I began.

Lola sat behind me. I was sure I could hear her heart beating. I was so overwhelmed by the row of photographers, I didn't dare look at them.

"Too often, we're treated as abstractions, faceless and nameless, subjects of debate rather than individuals with families, hopes, fears, and dreams," I went on, continuing to tell my story. The lies I had to tell so I could pass as an American. The sacrifices of my family: Lolo, Lola, and Mama, especially Mama. The generosity of Pat, Rich, and Jim, underscoring the all-too-forgotten reality that "there are countless other Jim Strands, Pat Hylands, and Rich Fischers of all backgrounds who stand alongside their undocumented neighbors," who don't need "pieces of paper—a passport or a green card—to treat us as human beings." I wasn't the only one who was done hiding. They were done hiding, too.

As I headed for the last few sentences of my prepared remarks, I grabbed my copy of President Kennedy's *A Nation of Immigrants*. The book's foreword was written by Ted Kennedy, his younger brother who fought for the passage of the 1965 Immigration and Nationality Act and, in turn, fought for immigration reform arguably harder than anyone else in the Senate. My family got here because of the 1965 law. I had hidden from Kennedy, too. While I was a reporter for the *Washington Post*, I interviewed him in Albuquerque in February 2008, a few days after he endorsed Obama for president. I wanted to tell him I was undocumented. I wanted to ask him for help. But I chickened out. I was not chickening out today.

I went off script.

"Before I take your questions here, I have a few of my own: what do you want to do with me?

"For all the undocumented immigrants who are actually sitting at this hearing, for all the people watching online, and for the eleven million of us: what do you want to do with us?

"And to me, the most important question, as a student of American history, is this: How do you define 'American'?"

As I ended my remarks, the only senator to ask a question was Sessions.

"Mr. Vargas, would you agree fundamentally that a great nation should have an immigration policy and then create a legal system that carries that policy out and then enforces that policy?"

"Yes, sir."

That was it. Faced with a real person, "a criminal alien," in his words, the kind whom he regularly describes as if he's talking about fungus in his toenail, that was his only question. Cruz wasn't even around; I don't think he heard the testimony. The silence from the other Republican senators who oppose any sort of reform, which they categorically call "amnesty," reminded me of the silence from the immigration officer I had called just a few months before.

I would find out that even though I publicly declared my undocumented status—on the phone, on TV shows, in front of Congress—I still did not exist in the eyes of ICE. Like most undocumented immigrants, I'd never been arrested. I'd been so careful not to get arrested. And that meant I'd never been in contact with ICE.

After all the years of lying, after all the years of trying to pass as an American, after all the anxiety, the uncertainty, the confusion, the only response I could get from the United States government, courtesy of the ICE agent who put me hold, was: "No comment."

How do you build a life with "no comment"?

2.

Home

I was stuck in traffic, one of those afternoon, bumper-to-bumper jams that Los Angeles is legendary for. Since my car was not moving anytime soon, I grabbed my iPhone and started scrolling through emails. I almost hit the gas and crashed into the Toyota Prius in front of me when I read the subject line: "Ready to buy a home?"

Is this a joke?

Is some divine, spiritual power trying to test me?

This was March 2017, at which point I had moved to Los Angeles. California had joined eleven other states (plus Washington, D.C.) in allowing their undocumented residents to apply for driver's licenses. I was renting a massive loft downtown, the largest place I'd ever lived in. Because I travel so much, because my life is in a packed suitcase, I had always had relatively small apartments. What's the point of having a home when you're never home? This time, I convinced myself that if I got a big-ass place and decorated it with all kinds of furniture and knickknacks, like a bookshelf made of wood and wire shaped like the USA, if I crowded the apartment with framed photographs of family and friends (a rare picture of Mama, Papa, and me together, celebrating my second birthday; a picture of Lolo, Lola, Uncle Conrad, and me in Zambales), if I hung up posters of Toni Morrison, James Baldwin, and Maya Angelou, who comprise what I consider my holy trinity of spiritual guidance, then maybe, just maybe, I would feel at home.

I opened the email, which turned out to be a promotional email from Bank of America's Home Loan Navigator. I've been a Bank of America customer since 1999, when Pat helped me open my only bank account. Since my life is dependent on and limited by government-issued IDs, I feel a special kind of ironic connection to my Bank of America debit card. It's the same reason I often use my American Express card and, whenever possible, fly on American Airlines.

I was so incensed and offended by the spam email that a few minutes later, I pulled over on the side of the freeway and called the number listed in the email.

I told the woman that asking me if I was ready to buy a home was cruel and unnecessary.

I told her that even though I didn't need a loan, that I've worked hard and have the means to put a down payment on a home, I couldn't buy a home because I didn't know anymore if this was my home.

I told her that I didn't know what else I had to do to prove to people that this is my home.

I told her that I could be deported at any time.

Her name was Paula. She cut me off.

"Mr. Vargas, what are you talking about?"

"I am undocumented. I don't have the right papers to be here."

"What do you mean? You're a Bank of America client. You're a longtime client."

She paused and, a few seconds later, asked, "Are you an illegal?"

There are many things this "illegal" cannot do.

I cannot vote. Which ID will I use to vote? My American Express card? Though I've lived in this country for twenty-five years, though I pay all kinds of taxes, which I am happy and willing to pay, since I am a product of public schools and public libraries, I have no voice in the democratic process. Think of it as taxation without legalization.

I cannot travel outside the United States. If I leave, there's no guarantee that I'd be allowed back.

I don't have access to Obamacare or any government-funded health program. In fact, even though I started and oversee a nonprofit organization that provides benefits and health insurance to seventeen full-time staffers, I have to buy my own private health insurance.

But as I get older, as the sense of isolation and invalidation digs deeper and deeper, I cannot bear to look myself in the face. Even though I am no longer hiding from the government, I am hiding from myself, all alone in a massive loft.

3.

Distant Intimacy

"You're really good at distant intimacy," a close friend (at least I thought we were close) once said to me.

I've spent my entire adult life separated from Mama because of walls and borders, never fully realizing that I've been putting up walls and delineating borders in all my relationships. With friends and mentors, I feel like I've dragged them into my mess. I was always a complicated problem with no easy solution.

Romantic entanglements are out of the question. I've never had a long-term boyfriend. During my summer internship in Philadelphia, I went out with a guy named Carmen, an Italian with an accent as thick as a milk shake. He was the first guy to ever tell me he loved me. The moment he said it—poof, I was gone. In my mind, boyfriends and long-term relationships require intimacy, not just physical but also emotional. I struggled with both. I don't like seeing myself naked, much less someone else seeing me naked. I've never looked at myself in a mirror completely naked. I'm no prude. It's not sex that I'm afraid of. It's the emotion that accompanies all but the most temporary of relationships that scares me. When someone tries to get close, I hide or run away. Or both.

I met "Roberto" at a party in D.C. in June 2012. We had dinner a couple of times, watched a movie once, and the flirtation got serious enough that he invited me to his apartment for Valentine's Day and asked that I spend the night. When I arrived, he was making chicken for dinner. He then handed me two thoughtful gifts: a bottle of vitamin gummy bears (he knew that I spend too much time flying and that I love gummy bears), and a book of poems by Pablo Neruda. I was so caught up in my own world that I didn't even think to bring him anything. After a few bites of the dinner he prepared, I told him I had to go. I grabbed my bag, headed to the door, and told him this was all too much.

The whole thing was terrifying. We were just getting to know each other, but already I was removing myself from the situation. Even if I stayed, I knew I would have to leave, because leaving, for me, was an inevitability. I couldn't bear the weight of that myself, much less impose it on someone else. Nothing was ever permanent, so I decided that leaving was better. *Nothing is better.* I thought coming out as undocumented, liberating myself from the lies and the need to pass, would make all of this better. I was wrong. Trading a private life that was in limbo for a public life that is still in limbo made it worse. In recent years, I've increasingly become a recluse, as if some part of me has already left, since I may have to leave anyway. I've started separating myself from people, even from my closest friends.

None closer than Jake.

I met Jake in 2007 at the Google headquarters, not too far from where I grew up. I was covering Ron Paul's visit with Googlers. Jake was there to see just how popular Paul was among young libertarians. (Very.) Jake worked at Idealist, a one-stop resource for jobs and internships in the nonprofit realm. As it happened, Jake was an idealist himself, the kind of guy who walked around like he had his own personal sunlight. To him, everything was good, positive, ideal. It would have been unbearable if he hadn't been so charming. I had just started my beat of covering the marriage of politics and technology, and Jake knew everyone who was anyone working in that emerging space. Though he was a Democrat, he hung around many Republicans. He even married a journalist and conservative commentator, Mary Katharine Ham. He was connected and he was a connector. Our friendship was sealed when he called me one very chilly night before the Iowa caucuses, and he coached me how to drive in the snow. "Dude, Jose, did you properly learn how to drive?"

Three years after we met, over lattes at Caribou Coffee near downtown Washington, I shared my secret. I told him about my plan to start an organization that collected the stories of undocumented immigrants. He was sold—even though, up until we met, he didn't know anyone who was undocumented.

"Jose was the gay, Filipino brother I never had, and I was the white, American-heartland brother he never had. An awesomely odd couple to be sure," Jake, who grew up in Tennessee, wrote on *HuffPost*. The headline: "My 'Illegal' Brother Defines American." Jake's outlook—the centrality of stories, the need for empathy, the importance of values as a way to connect with one another—was woven into the DNA of the organization.

Despite the fact that Jake had a full-time job in Washington—at that point he was helping run Change.org, the world's largest petition platform—he was just as committed to Define American. We were able to secure some funding and hire full-time staff. When we were looking for a campaign director, he recommended Ryan Eller, with whom he had previously worked at Change.org. Ryan, who was raised in Appalachia, is an expert digital organizer and all-around solid manager. An ordained Baptist minister, he lives in Kentucky. Together, we grew the organization, bringing on a diverse staff who looked like America, from different parts of the country. Whenever doubts clouded my mind, Jake was always my first call. I'd spent my entire life being obedient: good student, hardworking journalist, and now activist/advocate/whatever-this-was. I felt inadequate. He always told me I was enough, but I could never believe it.

Jake loved nature. Every time he asked me to go hiking, camping, fishing—or anything active that had to do with anything outdoors—I declined. One afternoon, after a fundraising meeting at my apartment, he started asking more personal questions about my family life and dating life. As usual, I brushed it all aside. "You know, you're gonna have to open up sometime," Jake said. "You can only push people away so many times."

He added: "Don't worry. You'll never push me away."

Jake was hit by a car while participating in a bike ride to

raise money for cancer research. The last time I saw Jake in person was at our dear friend Christina Bellantoni's wedding. One night months later, she called me in a panic. I couldn't understand what she was saying. "Jose, Jake is gone. Jose, Jake died." I was so sure it was mistake that I texted Jake. "Hey you there?"

That's the thing: he was always there, even when I didn't want him there, even when I kept pushing him away. On the night of the day he died, September 19, 2015, I stayed up all night waiting for him to show up, like an apparition. He was only thirty-four, just a few days older than me. I wanted to apologize for the all the times I was not present enough to see him, to thank him, to tell him I loved him. Since Jake's passing, Ryan and Christina, in their own ways, have tried to get closer, to fill some kind of space that Jake left.

Christina gave birth to a beautiful baby boy, Maxwell. Around his first birthday, I planned a visit to see him and spend time with Christina and her husband, Patrick. But I kept canceling and making up excuses. After a particularly terse and tense phone call, after yet another cancellation, Christina sent me an email:

"These years have not been easy for you, Jose. I know that. You are strong for others, and project strength day in and day out. But I know what you've lost, what you've given up, and how hard it is to live with such uncertainty.

What I can do is be there for you. Push you to let me—or someone—in, to help. Jake would want that, and you know he wouldn't back down, either, even if you got mad at him.

The only gift I ever want from you is to have you in my

life. And you're going to love this kid. He delivers pure joy and makes it look easy.

Your friend always, CB."

I don't know how many times I read that email. Each time I asked myself: When will I stop hiding and running away from people? What am I afraid of? Myself?

4.

Leaving

A few days before the inauguration of President Donald Trump, the building manager in the apartment complex I was living in—a nice guy named Mel, who cheered me on whenever he saw me on MSNBC, Fox News, or CNN—told me that if immigration agents showed up, he wasn't sure the building could hide me. He felt ashamed to say it, but tension had been building since the election. In a text message, Mel wrote: "It may be safer for you to move out." A lawyer friend of mine—I've collected a handful of lawyer friends since disclosing my status as an undocumented immigrant in 2011—suggested I prepare for the worst-case scenario. When I relayed that my building manager had asked that I consider moving out for my own safety, another lawyer friend replied, "Well, the man has a point. It's not a good idea for you to have a permanent address."

All around me, everyone issued warnings and raised red flags, especially after Trump signed executive orders on immigration, further confusing an already chaotic enforcement system and declaring every "illegal" a priority for deportation. One lawyer friend warned me against flying around the country, especially in the South and the Midwest. "God forbid you get detained in Ohio." Another lawyer friend insisted that I stop flying even within California, since news was spreading that immigration agents were checking the immigration status of domestic passengers. "Can you just stay put in one place," a lawyer friend asked, "and not fly around the country?"

Then Mony Ruiz-Velasco, a close friend and, yes, another lawyer, told me she didn't want me to stop flying, then made a bold suggestion: "What if you flew to Canada?" She texted me an article headlined, "Way More Migrants Are Now Sneaking Across the U.S.-Canada Border."

"Imagine the message you would send if you, of all people, decided to say, 'If you don't want me here, I'm moving to Canada!'"

I entertained the idea for about two weeks.

I love Canada, or at least the Canada of my imagination, which is wrapped in all things *Anne of Green Gables*. I entertained the idea enough to look for apartments in Toronto, and was surprised that rent in Canada's biggest city seemed far more affordable than rents I'd paid in Washington, D.C., New York City, San Francisco, and Los Angeles. I took it seriously enough that I told Ryan and Bích Ngọc Cao, the top two leaders at Define American, that they should prepare for a scenario in which I am not physically somewhere in the U.S. to help run Define American. (Whatever reservations Ryan and Bích Ngọc had, personal and professional, they never shared them. In a conference call discussing the possibility of my moving to Canada, Ryan suggested we think about reaching out to the office of Justin Trudeau.) I took it seriously enough that I told Ate Gladys. Gladys is that relative in your family that you trust with everything—every secret, every fear, every insecurity. She has witnessed how difficult and disorienting the past few years have been for me, the cost of the relentless pull from all kinds of people.

And what exacerbates the whole situation is the constant worrying of my Filipino family. If Trump ordered my deportation, I would not be safe in the Philippines, led by President Rodrigo Duterte, whose hatred of journalists is just as notorious as Trump's. Shortly after the election, Ate Gladys was browsing through tweets directed at me and found a troubling image. Someone actually took the time to Photoshop the famous photograph of a South Vietnamese police chief killing a Vietcong suspect into Trump pointing a gun to my face as a smiling Duterte looks on.

Ate Gladys's reaction to the idea of my moving to Canada unnerved me. Above all, she seemed relieved.

"I want you to relax, to build a home," she said. "I want you to stop running around."

My thirty-sixth birthday was approaching, another year of being stuck in America. Since many assume I'm Mexican, I figured I should at least see Mexico, which is less than three hundred miles away from my apartment in downtown Los Angeles. But of course I couldn't go. I tried not using the word "stuck," but a careful review of my thesaurus yielded no suitable alternative. The word was "stuck," and I was stuck. Anne Shirley's Canada seemed like a way out.

Three days after my birthday, on the morning of Monday, February 6, 2017, an email landed in my inbox. In all

caps, its subject line read: "LEADER NANCY PELOSI
INVITATION - JOINT SESSION OF CONGRESS."

> Dear Jose,
>
> Good morning! Leader Nancy Pelosi invites you to be her
> guest at the Joint Session of Congress by the President
> on Tuesday, February 28th, 2017 at the United States
> Capitol.

I first met Nancy Pelosi when she was Speaker of the
House and I was a political reporter for the *Washington Post*.
While I was a student at San Francisco State, I lived in Pelosi's
district. Her invitation did not come lightly. Pelosi knew what
she was asking for and what my presence inside the Capitol
would mean.

I forwarded her invitation to a few lawyer friends, all
of whom advised against accepting it. ("What would be the
point? Aren't you thinking about Canada?" many wondered.)
Alida Garcia, another lawyer friend, who had worked for the
Obama campaign, was so strongly against accepting that she
fired off an email in the early hours of the morning:

> Jose,
>
> I'm not saying don't do it, these are just things worth
> considering:
>
> - Their goal is to scare people to self-deport, a part
>   of that is deporting someone that sends chills down
>   people's spines to encourage them to leave. If you
>   can't find a way out of enforcement, others can't.
>
> - Nancy Pelosi is arguably the most GOP antagonizing
>   figure in the entire United States Congress and you

would be her guest. People aren't trying to work in collaboration with Nancy Pelosi should something bad happen.

- You'll be on federal property, in a publicized defined place, and while DC is moving to a sanctuary I'm pretty sure jurisdictionally they could just get some kind of warrant and have someone come grab you at the Capitol.

- You may provoke them in a way that doesn't result in harming you but harms others because they don't want the community to feel proud.

- Raids are already happening all over the place.

- General Kelly [then the secretary of the Department of Homeland Security] believes in enforcing the law. I don't think he wants to unnecessarily harm people or have big public blowouts of things, but if the law says you should be deported, he's going to use that as an excuse to deport you is my instinct.

- You are poking the bear. I recognize you poke the collective bear for a living but this is a different bear.

- It took .25 seconds for the Breitbart website to pull up 725 articles under the search "Jose Antonio Vargas." Breitbart runs immigration policy in the United States.

You don't have to be a hero. You don't owe people shit. If this feels in your heart that this is what YOU have to do for YOU as well—then it's worth considering. But just because an opportunity arises to be defiant doesn't mean you're the only one out of 11 million people who has to do it.

5.
Staying

The first time I understood what Washington, D.C., represented—the physical and symbolic distance between the White House and the U.S. Capitol—was when I watched *The American President*. Michael Douglas, playing the fictional President Andrew Shepard, gave a galvanizing speech that I committed to memory: "America isn't easy. America is advanced citizenship. You've gotta want it bad, 'cause it's gonna put up a fight."

Pelosi's formal invitation, and Alida's carefully considered note, put my predicament in sharp focus. It was clarifying. I came to the realization that I refuse to let a presidency scare me from my own country. I refuse to live a life of fear defined by a government that doesn't even know why it fears what it fears. Because I am not a citizen by law or by birth, I've had to create and hold on to a different kind of citizenship. Not exactly what President Shepard described as "advanced citizenship"—I don't know what that meant—but something more akin to what I call citizenship of participation. Citizenship is showing up. Citizenship is using your voice while making sure you hear other people around you. Citizenship is how you live your life. Citizenship is resilience.

I accepted the invitation. And in the spirit of "radical transparency," I wrote an essay for the *Post*, the same newspaper that had killed my coming-out essay six years before. This time, the essay was published a few minutes after I entered the Capitol and sat down in the gallery of the House's hallowed chamber.

I explained why I showed up:

I decided to show up tonight because that's what immigrants, undocumented and documented, do: We show up. Despite the obvious risks and palpable fear, we show up to work, to school, to church, to our communities, in big cities and rural towns. We show up and we participate. This joint session of Congress is a quintessential American moment at a critical juncture in our history. I am honored to attend and remind our elected leaders and everyone watching that immigration, at its core, is about families and love—the sacrifices of our families, and the love that we feel for a country we consider our home although it labels us "aliens." We show up even though we're unwanted, even when most Americans don't understand.... why we come here in the first place....We show up even though many Americans, especially white Americans with their own immigrant backgrounds, can't seem to see the common threads between why we show up and why they showed up, at a time when showing up did not require visas and the Border Patrol didn't exist yet.

After attending the joint session—and after many conversations with lawyer friends—I moved out of my apartment in Los Angeles. I put most everything I own in storage and started giving away furniture to relatives and friends. For the first time since leaving Lolo and Lola's house after my high school graduation, I don't have my own apartment. I don't have a permanent address. I'm staying at hotels, Airbnbs, and in spare bedrooms of close friends.

I've decided to keep my travel schedule as is, fully aware of the possible consequences.

I don't know what it's like to be deported.

But I do know what it's like to be arrested and detained.

6.
Detained

Of all the ways I imagined the inevitable, I never envisioned sitting on the cold cement floor of a jail cell in south Texas surrounded by children.

It was July 2014. The cell, as I remember it, was no bigger than twenty feet by thirty feet. All around me were about twenty-five boys, as young as five years old, the oldest no more than twelve. The air reeked of body odor. A boy across the room from me was crying inconsolably, his head buried on his chest. I tried to make eye contact to no avail. Most of the boys wore dazed expressions. It was clear they had no idea where they were or why they were there.

The only source of wonder came from Mylar blankets, the flimsy metallic sheets that were supposed to keep us warm, the same blankets that were first used in outer space, which must be as desolate as this cell. By the look of it, the boys had never seen these blankets before and didn't know what to do with them. Three boys played with a blanket like it was a toy, crunching it up into a ball, passing it back and forth.

A window faced a central area where a dozen or so patrol agents were stationed, but there was no view of the outside world. All I could do was stare at the boys' shoes. My shoes were shiny and brand-new, theirs dirty, muddy, and worn down. The only thing our shoes had in common was that none of them had laces.

"Jose Antonio Vargas," said an agent as he walked in.

Startled, I sprung up, unsure why my name was being called.

"I don't need you. Not yet," the agent said. "But we're gonna move you."

Before he could hear me ask why, the agent shut the door as another detainee, a young woman with a wide-eyed baby on her hip, walked by, unaccompanied.

The moment the agent said my name, one of the boys playing with a blanket started speaking to me. I had no idea what he was saying. The one word I could make out was "*miedo.*" Something about "*miedo.*"

If I spoke Spanish, I could have told the boys not to be scared.

If I spoke Spanish, I could have told the boys about Ellis Island. About how the very first person in line on the opening day of America's first immigration station—an unaccompanied minor named Annie Moore who traveled on a steamship from Ireland—was someone just like them. Except she was white, before she knew she was white.

If I spoke Spanish, I could have told the boys that none of this was their fault. I could have made sure they understood—even if most Americans do not—that people like us come to America because America was in our countries.

I could have explained, in the clearest, most accessible way I could, the connection between the irreversible actions of the United States of America and the inevitable reactions in their countries of birth. How the push-and-pull factors of our migration are way more complicated than the need to take a picture at the foot of the Statue of Liberty. How the largest groups of people who migrate to the U.S.A.— voluntarily, forcibly, unknowingly, like them—do so because of what the U.S. government has done to their countries. How a trade agreement, like the North American Free Trade Agreement, drove millions of Mexicans out of jobs and led parents to cross borders and climb up walls so they could feed their kids. How six decades of interventionist policies by both Republicans and Democrats brought economic and political instability and sowed violence in El Salvador, Guatemala, and Honduras. If I spoke Spanish, I could have explained, in the clearest, most accessible way I could, the connection between the dirty, muddy, worn-out Reeboks and Nikes they were wearing inside that cell and the inherent American need to expand its economic and political empire. I could have drawn a line between what used to be called "imperialism"—justified by "Manifest Destiny," "the White Man's Burden," and America's desire to "discover" new "frontiers"—to what is now known as "internationalism" and "globalization."

I first encountered Rudyard Kipling's "The White Man's Burden" while reading James Baldwin's *The Fire Next Time,* not knowing that the "silent, sullen peoples" whom Kipling describes as "half devil and half child" were Filipinos. I didn't know that Kipling wrote the poem to urge Americans to do what the British, the Spanish, and all the European countries had already done: take the "burden" of empire. The subtitle of the poem, in fact, is *"The United States and the Philippine Islands."*

I don't understand Spanish. The only Spanish thing about me is my name. Aside from asking *"Dondé esta la biblioteca?"* ("Where is the library?"), one of a few phrases I know is *"No hablo español."* ("I don't speak Spanish.") I told the boy: *"No hablo español."* Quickly, I added, *"Soy filipino."* I am Filipino: a declaration that seemed to cause more confusion to the young boy holding the crunched-up blanket. I'm not sure he heard me when I said, almost in a whisper, like a prayer, *"Pepeton ang pangalan ko."* My name is Pepeton.

It's my nickname, combining the nicknames of Jose (Pepe) and Antonio (Ton). But it's more than a sobriquet, more than a term of endearment. It's the name of my past: what Mama and everyone in the Philippines who knows me calls me. It's the name I don't tell people about, certainly not after I found out I was in America without proper documents. It's the name I've avoided so I could construct a different kind of identity, not the "illegal immigrant" you see and hear about in the news, but a successful journalist who breaks news and writes about the news. It's the name I've escaped from so I could escape whatever and whomever I needed to escape: my past and Mama, the U.S. government, myself. But there was no place to hide now, nothing to run away from, no role to play.

All I could see as I stared at the boys was young Pepeton staring back at me.

7.

The Machine

To understand how the boys and I ended up inside that jail cell, you must unravel a vast enforcement apparatus that is part police force, part frontier cavalry, part deportation machine, and altogether unprecedented in immigration history. For the most part, it's also been largely unheralded, hiding in plain sight for the past quarter century as cries of "Build the wall!" got louder and louder. This apparatus grew in the 1990s, its predatory arms extending their reach after the 9/11 attacks.

The gruesome attacks on 9/11, carried out by foreigners who legally immigrated to the country on temporary visas, proved to be a turning point. As our country geared up to fight the "war on terror," immigration was wedded to terrorism. That was the clear message from the Bush administration, which shuttered the eighty-four-year-old Immigration and Naturalization Service (INS) and replaced it with the Department of Homeland Security, whose chief task was protecting Americans from terrorists. And that insidious message—the narrative of immigrants as potential terrorists, a threat to our national security—blanketed news coverage.

Around the same time my mother in the Philippines sent me to California to live with Lolo and Lola, in the mid-1990s, the federal government moved to control the border. My first few years in America were the "tough-on-crime" years as defined by President Clinton and the lawmakers who were part of the Republican Revolution that swept Congress. Getting "tough on crime" led to getting tough on "criminal aliens," which turned out to be a bipartisan affair.

In 1994 Pete Wilson, the Republican governor of California, championed the successful Proposition 187 ballot initiative, which aimed to ban "illegal aliens" from using nonemergency health care, public education, and other services. Not to be outflanked on the right, Clinton launched "Operation Gatekeeper" in the same year, its mission to regain control of "the borders," particularly the San Diego–Tijuana border, at that point the busiest land crossing in the world. New miles of fencing were built. Hundreds of new agents were trained. The budget of the Border Patrol, which fell under the INS, doubled. Though the Clinton administration declared victory, the policy was considered a failure. The only success, if you can call it that, was shifting illegal crossings from the suburbs of San Diego and El Paso toward treacherous mountains and deserts.

Egged on by congressional Republicans, Clinton deepened the damage, signing two omnibus bills that laid the groundwork for an enforcement apparatus that has only grown under every subsequent president, Republican or Democrat. Two years after signing a "crime bill," and fresh on the heels of signing "welfare reform," Clinton signed the Illegal Immigration Reform and Immigrant Responsibility

Act and the Antiterrorism and Effective Death Penalty Act in 1996. Together, these two bills made it easier to criminalize and deport all immigrants, documented and undocumented, and made it harder for undocumented immigrants like me to adjust our status and "get legal."

Before 1996, immigrants, regardless of status, could get deported following state or federal conviction for murder, rape, or other serious felonies.

Since 1996, immigrants, regardless of legal status, can get deported for theft, counterfeiting, or possession of stolen property, among other relatively minor offenses.

Before 1996, immigrants who had been living in the U.S. for at least seven years, were of "good moral character," and were "conviction-free" could get legal status if they showed that deportation would cause them or their lawfully present relatives "extreme hardship."

Since 1996, a process called "expedited removal" empowers immigration agents to deport immigrants without bringing them before an immigration judge for a hearing if said immigrants cannot prove that they have been in the country for two years. What's more, the majority of undocumented immigrants cannot adjust their status and "get legal" even if they marry a U.S. citizen or qualify for a green card because of a relative. I've met dozens of undocumented men—it's always been men—who are married to U.S. citizen women but can't adjust their status. Worst of all, undocumented immigrants are banished for at least three years if they've lived in the country without proper documentation for six months; if they've been here illegally for a year or more, the banishment lasts ten years.

Taken together, these bills not only expanded the criteria for who can get detained and deported, they also expanded the population of immigrants who couldn't adjust their status, leading them to fear detention and deportation at any point. It's a government-created, taxpayer-funded catch-22, and we're all tied up in it like a Gordian knot. If I chose to leave and go back to the Philippines, then I'd face a ten-year ban on reentry into the U.S., since I've been living illegally in the U.S. for twenty-five years. And even if I returned to my country of birth, there's no guarantee I'd ever be allowed back to the country I call my home. Put simply, for the government, keeping people "illegal" is much easier than allowing them to get "legal." Perhaps it's no accident that the ITIN, which allows undocumented workers to pay federal taxes, was created in 1996.

As the years wore on, the enforcement apparatus locked up more and more people, spending billions in the process. Since the Clinton era, detainment became mandatory for certain immigrants, including asylum seekers and those with criminal records, however minor the offenses. Immigrants filled detention beds in prisons and jails across the country, many of them private, for-profit facilities. The average daily number of immigrants locked in detention skyrocketed after Clinton left office. A detention bed quota of thirty-four thousand immigrants on a daily basis was established during the Obama administration. At that time, no other law enforcement agency was subjected to a daily statutory quota.

If we are not detaining immigrants, we are deporting them. According to the nonpartisan Migration Policy Institute, our country went from deporting seventy thousand immigrants in 1996 to removing four hundred thousand per year through the first term of the Obama administration. Though activists and advocacy groups have branded Obama as "Deporter-in-Chief," the number of deportations started increasing during the Bush era because of a program called Operation Streamline.

Under Operation Streamline, border crossers approach a judge in small groups, no more than seven or eight, their bodies shackled and chained. Their prison sentences range from days to months or years. As documented in the book *Indefensible: A Decade of Mass Incarceration of Migrants Prosecuted for Crossing the Border,* by Judith A. Greene, Bethany Carson, and Andrea Black, almost a quarter of people locked up by the Federal Bureau of Prisons in 2015 were noncitizens, most of them charged for illegal entry or illegal reentry. Locking up people for the "crime" of improper migration is overcrowding federal prisons, worsening our mass incarceration problem.

The cost of enforcing our laws and protecting our borders is almost astronomically absurd. A 2014 article published in *Politico* found that the U.S. government spends more money each year on border and immigration enforcement than the combined budgets of the Federal Bureau of Investigation, the Bureau of Alcohol, Tobacco, Firearms and Explosives, the Drug Enforcement Administration, the Secret Service, and the U.S. Marshals. Altogether, the article noted that more than $100 billion of our tax dollars has been spent on border and immigration control since 9/11. And these numbers preceded the Trump era, with President Obama spending record sums on immigration enforcement even as he championed a broader legislative solution that neither political party had been able to deliver.

Customs and Border Protection (CBP), the country's largest law enforcement agency, employs an estimated sixty thousand people and operates a fleet of about 250 planes, helicopters, and drones, making it the largest law enforcement air force in the world. The Border Patrol, which is part of CBP, uses a "digital wall" comprising eight thousand cameras to monitor our southern border and ports of entries, and employs 18,500 agents on the nearly two-thousand-mile-long U.S.-Mexico border. Extending from California to Texas, about seven hundred miles of fencing that includes wire mesh, chain link, post and rail, sheet piling, and concrete barriers has been constructed at a cost of between $2.8 million and $3.9 million per mile.

And all for what?

To protect Americans from whom?

8.

National Security Threat

What transpired in the summer of 2014 epitomizes the moral bankruptcy that characterizes how we talk about immigration in America during the first two decades of the twenty-first century. Headlines from even reputable news organizations like CBS News read: "Is the Surge of Illegal Child Immigrants a National Security Threat?"

A couple of days after I read that CBS News story, Cristina Jiménez of United We Dream, a national youth-led immigrant rights organization, sent me a text message, asking if Define American would be interested in joining a delegation traveling to McAllen, Texas, in the Rio Grande Valley. Among the longest rivers in North America, the Rio Grande marks the official border between Mexico and the U.S. Following America's victory in the Mexican-American War in 1848, the Treaty of Guadalupe Hidalgo gave the U.S. the Rio Grande as a boundary for Texas, not to mention ownership of California and a vast terrain that included most of Utah, Nevada, and Arizona and parts of Wyoming and Colorado, all for the price of fifteen million dollars. When you meet Mexicans who say that the border crossed them, this is what they mean.

The goal of the trip, Cristina said, was to organize a vigil welcoming arriving Central American refugees, most of whom were children fleeing for their lives. Many traveled alone, a journey of hundreds of miles by trains, buses, and on foot just to get across the Rio Grande. Unavoidably, the Rio Grande became ground zero for political posturing, attracting the conservative firebrand Sean Hannity, who taped his Fox News show on the banks of the river. Republicans including Rick Perry, the Texas governor, blamed the "border crisis" on DACA, the program that gives temporary legal status to undocumented immigrants brought to the U.S. as children. But as congressional Democrats and the Obama administration pointed out, the unaccompanied minors did not qualify for DACA. What they did quality for, according to human rights experts, was refugee status—something President Obama was careful not to give them. The politics of immigration was so poisonous even helpless kids couldn't be seen as kids. When Hillary Clinton, a longtime champion of children's rights, was asked to weigh in, she said tens of thousands of children and teenagers should be sent back to their home countries. "We have to send a clear message: just because your child gets across the border doesn't mean your child gets to stay," Clinton said at a CNN-hosted town hall.

Whether you call them migrants, immigrants, or refugees, their journeys included an arduous trek through blistering desert terrain. Often, they lacked food, water, and shelter. Many arrived dehydrated and hungry. Some required medical attention. Once they crossed the Rio Grande, they didn't try to hide from Border Patrol agents. They walked up to the officers and gave themselves up.

I wasn't sure if I should fly to Texas. I was not a refugee. I wondered if my showing up there would take attention away from their plight. But the more I read about what was happening in McAllen, the more I wanted to go. My dear friend Paola Mendoza, a Colombian-born filmmaker who has made immigration central to her art, suggested that we film the vigil. My plan was to fly in, participate in the vigil, help Paola with the filming, and fly out. I'd never been to southern Texas. My only experience of being close to the border was in Southern California, where some of my relatives live. The Texas border was a whole other experience, a militarized occupied territory swarming with Border Patrol agents, Department of Public Safety officers, and immigration officials. Along the three-mile drive from the McAllen Miller International Airport, where I was picked up, to my hotel, I counted seven Border Patrol cars, just driving around. Nearby, a Department of Public Safety helicopter hovered. At the Starbucks not too far from the hotel, many of the customers were uniformed agents and officers on their breaks.

When my friend Mony, an immigration lawyer who used to work in the area, saw on my Facebook page that I was in McAllen, she texted me: "I am so glad you are visiting the kids near the border. But how will you get through the checkpoint on your way back?" A curious question, I thought, and one I dismissed. I've visited the border before, in California. What checkpoint? What was she talking about?

Then Tania Chavez, an undocumented youth leader from the Minority Affairs Council, one of the organizers of the vigil, asked me the same question: "How will you get out of here?" Tania grew up in this border town. As the day wore on, as the reality sank in, Tania spelled it out for me: You might not get through airport security, where CPB also checks for IDs, and you will definitely not get through the immigration checkpoints set up within forty-five miles of this border town. At these checkpoints, you will be asked for documentation. "Even if you tell them you're a U.S. citizen, they will ask you follow-up questions if they don't believe you," Tania told me.

When I told Cristina about the situation, her eyes widened. "Oh my God, Jose! I forgot you don't have DACA!"

At the Texas border, "border security" is an inescapable daily reality, a physical and existential reminder of where you cannot go, what your limitations are. "Border security" means running random checkpoints anywhere within one hundred miles of the U.S.-Mexico border, a Constitution-free zone in which agents can stop your car, inspect your belongings, and ask for your papers, regardless of your immigration status. (The Fourth Amendment does not allow for citizens to be subjected to random search and seizures, but in the interest of "national security," the Fourth Amendment does not apply within a hundred miles of the border.) For residents of the Rio Grande Valley who are undocumented, or who are U.S. citizens but live with parents or siblings who are undocumented, "border security" means knowing you can't drive for more than half an hour south, no more than an hour and a half east, and no more than two hours north.

Soon Cristina was strategizing on how I could leave McAllen quietly and discreetly. She kept apologizing for not remembering that I didn't have DACA. "We need to get you out," she texted. "We can drive you to SA." San Antonio.

Someone suggested hiding me in the trunk so I could get through the checkpoint.

The moment that suggestion was made—hide? in the trunk?—I knew in my heart that I had to stay. Paola agreed with me. "This happened for a reason, Jose," she said. "You are stuck here for a reason." I called Ryan and told him what was happening. I texted Alida: "I'm in McAllen and I'm stuck." Within hours, Ryan and Alida decided to fly to McAllen, just so they could be with me regardless of what happened. I decided to continue what I've been doing since I stopped hiding who I am. To practice "radical transparency," I wrote an essay that was published on *Politico* the following day:

"I write this from the city of McAllen. . . . In the last 24 hours I realize that, for an undocumented immigrant like me, getting out of a border town in Texas—by plane or by land— won't be easy. It might, in fact, be impossible."

The headline: "Trapped on the Border."

Some people thought the whole thing was a stunt, including activists in the immigrant rights movement. "He's just trying to take away from the kids," a Dreamer I knew posted on Facebook, and since we were friends, I saw his post. My stomach dropped. It was an accident. I didn't know I was going to be cornered there. I had to call Lola and assure her everything would be fine. I drafted an email to my loved ones and explained what was happening and what could happen. After consulting with immigration lawyers, we decided that I would leave McAllen in the same way I arrived: by plane. A wealthy friend offered to get me a private plane, which I thought was a joke until he assured me it wasn't. I declined the offer and said I wanted to fly out how I flew in. Alida volunteered to accompany me at the airport. She and I would be on the same flight. With the help of Lara Drasin and Maria Cruz Lee, my colleagues at Define American, Ryan was prepared for all possible scenarios.

I flew into McAllen from John F. Kennedy International Airport in New York City, where I used my Philippine passport—the only piece of acceptable identification I had at the time—to get through security. Like all the other airports across the country that I had flown into and out of, there was no Border Patrol agent checking papers of domestic travelers at JFK. The McAllen airport was different. At the McAllen airport, a Border Patrol agent would stand next to the TSA agent checking everyone's papers. So, as Alida and I waited in line, I inserted my Philippine passport inside my pocket copy of the Declaration of Independence and U.S. Constitution, as if that act provided some sort of protection. My heart pounded in my chest as I approached the agents, as my mind cataloged every possible outcome.

A TSA agent checked my passport and compared it to my plane ticket. Then a Border Patrol agent took my passport from the TSA agent and flipped it open.

"Do you have your visa?" the agent asked.

"No, there's no visa," I replied matter-of-factly, as if I was writing a news article and answering the question for someone else.

The moment he asked, "Are you here illegally?" I reminded myself that it was me he was talking to.

Without any hesitation, I answered with a clipped "Yes."

Then, in a clear voice drenched in defiance, I added: "I am."

9.

Alone

The agents inside the sixty-eight-thousand-square-foot McAllen Border Patrol Station on West Military Highway did not know what to do with me.

They kept moving me from one cell to another. An agent took me out of the cell with the boys and put me in a much smaller one by myself. Then back again with the boys, then back again to the cell by myself. I realized that I was separated from the other men, who were locked up in different cells. I walked past one cell that had only grown women—pregnant women, women cradling babies, women talking to one another.

Two hours passed before an agent opened the door and peeked his head in. "Are you famous or something?" He closed the door and seconds later opened it again. He held up his phone and showed me an article on CNN. "Dude, you're all over the news."

After I was handcuffed at the airport, I'd been driven alone in a white van. The ride to the station took less than fifteen minutes, if that. Upon my arrival, two agents took everything I had: my phone, my wallet, my backpack, my luggage. I was asked to take off my leather belt and the laces in my shoes. When I asked why, one of the agents said, "We don't want you hurting yourself."

I wanted to laugh out loud after the agent said that. I've always used laughter to conceal the pain; here, to distance and detach myself from the absurdity of this whole ordeal. Is this really about who has the right papers and what the laws are? Or is this about someone to control? Is this really about who is a citizen or not? Are we talking about the same citizenship that many Americans callously take for granted? Are these agents so blithely unaware that they and their government have hurt me more than I could ever hurt myself?

But I said nothing.

There was no bathroom in the cell. You had to call an agent to use one. Incredibly, I did not use the bathroom in the hours I was locked up. I managed to hold it in. I should have used the bathroom as an excuse to check out the rest of the station. That was what a curious and enterprising reporter would have done. But for the first time in my adult life, I wasn't a reporter, which was the only thing I knew how to be, so long as I was reporting on other people and what was happening to them. I was something else altogether, someone I didn't entirely recognize.

The quietness is forbidding, all alone in that cell. Nothing but you and your thoughts, which become somewhat tangible, bouncing around the white walls and the cold floors before building into some emotional squall. There was no place to run. No role to play. Though I was fully clothed, I'd never felt more naked in my whole life.

My life of deadlines came to a halt, the facts clearly in front of me. The father I never had, or who left me, the mother I left, or who left me. The country I left, which was my home, which I don't know much about, and the country I am in, which is my home, except it isn't. It's dangerous out there, and home should be the place where we feel safe and at peace.

Home is not something I should have to earn.

Humanity is not some box I should have to check.

It occurred to me that I'd been in an intimate, long-term relationship all along. I was in a toxic, abusive, codependent relationship with America, and there was no getting out.

The very reason that I'm locked up in this cell is because of who I am and who I've become. Who am I without America? What would I be without America?

Sitting alone in that cell, I concluded that none of this was an accident. None of it. You know how politicians and the news media that cover them like to say that we have a "broken immigration system"? Inside that cell I came to the conclusion that we do not have a broken immigration system. We don't. What we're doing—waving a "Keep Out!" flag at the Mexican border while holding up a "Help Wanted" sign a hundred yards in—is deliberate. Spending billions building fences and walls, locking people up like livestock, deporting people to keep the people we don't want out, tearing families apart, breaking spirits—all of that serves a purpose. People are forced to lie, people spend years if not decades passing in some kind of purgatory. And step by step, this immigration system is set up to do exactly what it does.

Dear America, is this what you really want? Do you even know what is happening in your name?

I don't know what else you want from us.

I don't know what else you need us to do.

10.

Interview

"So when did you arrive in the United States?"

After the sixth hour, I was taken out of the cell and escorted inside an office, where an agent asked me questions while he filled out a form. His name was Mario, and he was clean shaven and young-looking, as if he'd graduated from high school just few years before. He was of Mexican descent, like all the other agents in the station.

"August 3, 1993."

"Did you cross the border?"

"No. My border was the Pacific Ocean."

"Huh?"

"I'm from the Philippines."

He laughed. "Hey, I know someone from the Philippines. You guys have Mexican names." As he started talking about "Pac Man"—as in Manny Pacquiao, the famous Filipino boxer—I saw him place an accent on the "é" in "José." I stopped him and said that Filipinos, for reasons I don't fully understand, don't put accents on our Spanish names. "I guess it's our way of rebelling against Spanish colonialism. Or something like that." I might not be able to control what was happening, but I was going to control the punctuation of my name. It was a defense mechanism, also a way of distracting myself from the fact that I was losing control. Usually I ask questions. I don't answer them.

Later, I would find out why my name doesn't carry an accent mark. After the Americans forced the Spanish out of the Philippines, their typewriters couldn't type accented vowels. My name is Jose because of Spanish colonialism. But Jose isn't José because of American imperialism. Even my name isn't really mine.

He broke the silence and asked: "Who did you come with? Your mom?"

"No. My mom put me on a plane."

"By yourself?"

"No. I was with this guy who my mom told me was an uncle."

"So you came with your uncle."

"Actually, I found out later on that he wasn't my uncle. He was a stranger that my grandfather—my Mama's dad—paid to get me here. My mother sent me to live with her parents—"

He cut me off. "You came with a coyote," he said. "A lot of the kids here had coyotes."

I nodded.

More silence.

Again, he broke it and asked: "What do you do?"

"I'm a journalist."

"Yeah. I know. I looked you up," he said. "Why journalist?"

"I don't know." By this point, I was annoyed and confused. He already knew I was a journalist, yet he asked the question just to stall the conversation, like he needed to buy some time. He kept looking at the window waiting for someone important to show up.

"You always wanted to be a journalist?"

"No. I wanted to make films." If he had looked even remotely interested, I would have said that I wanted to make films because it was a way of showing the world what you see, like the Paris of François Truffaut and the Rome of Federico Fellini. Films are a way of seeing beyond yourself, into other people and other places. Films are possibilities, both real and imagined.

Instead, I continued: "When I found out I was undocumented, that I didn't have the right kind of papers to be here, I wanted my name to be in the newspaper." If he really wanted to know, I would have said that having my name in the newspaper—"by Jose Antonio Vargas"—was the only way I could think of existing and contributing something concrete in the process. That was my article. I reported it. I wrote it. It's real. I'm real.

This time I broke the silence. "Why did you become a Border Patrol agent?"

"The benefits are solid, man."

Seconds later, another guard came into the room, the same guard who took my shoelaces and asked if I was famous. All afternoon, the guards I'd encountered had given me knowing looks, like I was a lab experiment they had figured out. If they had, they didn't tell me. Who was I? Who had I become? Where was I going? What they did say was that within an hour or so, I would be released, but they were trying to figure out how. I kept asking why I was being released.

They wouldn't say. "There are a lot of reporters out there," the other guard said. "They're waiting for you." I asked if either of them spoke Spanish. They both did.

"What's *'miedo'*?"

"Fear," one of the agents said. "It means fear."

11.

Cycle of Loss

Sitting on the floor, staring at the boys in the cell, I kept thinking of their parents, the fear they must have felt knowing that they needed to do what they needed to do. I also kept thinking of my mother, wondering as I had so many times over all these years what she told herself as she said goodbye to me at that airport twenty-five years ago.

Mama and I rarely talked about what happened at the airport. Sometimes I would ask about a fact here or there. What was I wearing? What was she wearing? What were her last words to me? But we never talked about how we felt, what we lost, what it means. That's the truth, as hard as it may seem to believe. Maybe it's because it's too hard for me to ask and too painful for her to remember. Maybe it's because we both know it wouldn't change anything. Maybe it's because the truth is too heavy to carry around.

The truth is, I'm not the only one who lost a mother. Mama lost a mother, too. Lola, my mother's mother, left the Philippines and moved to America in 1984, three years after I was born. Lola had seen her only daughter, my mama, no more than six times in thirty-four years, quick visits of two to three weeks every few years. Mama is waiting in line to legally come to America. As the decades have passed, their relationship, like my relationship with Mama, is mostly transactional, measured by the American products that we ship over to the Philippines and the U.S. dollars that we provide that Mama can't live without. We think we can bury what we've lost under all the things we can buy. When the truth is, the loss that my mother can't express to her mother is what I struggle to express to her now.

The truth is, if Mama had known then what she knows now—that calling her on the phone is difficult, because I can't really pretend that I know the voice on the other end of the line—that seeing her on Skype or FaceTime feels like some sort of twisted joke, exposing the reality that the technology that easily connects us has rendered the very borders that divide us even more visible—I'm not sure if she would have said goodbye at the airport. On one of our rare phone calls she said, "I look at you, now, the person you've become, and how can I have any regrets." I'm sure she meant it as a statement, but it sounded like a question.

The truth is, there's a part of me, I'm uncertain how much, who is still in that airplane, wondering why Mama put me there.

12.
Truth

Speaking of the truth, for years now, I haven't wanted to find out exactly how I got out of detention on July 15, 2014. For a person who's made a life out of asking questions, I didn't want to face the facts.

I didn't want to know that while most undocumented immigrants are arrested, detained, and deported, without due process, I was able to get out after eight hours of being locked up.

I didn't want to know that friends who had connections to the Philippine Embassy in the U.S. called the consul general and got him to call DHS to point out that I was Filipino. At the time, the detention centers in Texas were so packed that agents were doing what were called "drag and drops"— dropping you across the border right into Mexico.

I didn't want to know that the reason why the agents kept moving me from cell to cell was because journalists and photographers were scheduled to tour the station that day— the same day I happened to be locked up. Agents didn't want journalists to see me locked up in a cell with the boys.

I didn't want to know that the moment I was arrested at the airport, friends called their contacts at DHS and the White House. People in positions of power responded and offered help. Even though I didn't want to know, I knew I needed to know, however belatedly.

In the process of finishing this book, of cracking open my life so I could put it back together, I called Mama. We spoke longer than we'd ever spoken, telling each other things we've avoided in the twenty-five years we've grown apart. Mama will turn sixty-one this year. At thirty-seven, I am a year older than she was when she dropped me off at the airport on that hurried morning. I told her that since that morning, I've always been hurried, that working on this book is the first time I've ever allowed myself the space and time to feel, and that I'd been feeling lost and alone. When she asked me where I was, I said I was staying at a hotel. I told her I had no home at the moment: no physical space of my own, no permanent address.

"Maybe," Mama said, her voice growing fainter for a moment, "maybe it's time to come home."

Acknowledgments

There is nothing greater than gratitude, and my profound thanks to the people who made this book possible, especially the people who bring life to book publishing.

Thank you, Jennifer Rudolph Walsh and Jay Mandel, my agents at WME, who propelled me to start the writing process, which meant asking myself hard questions. Thank you to my editor Julia Cheiffetz, who for years believed that I had a book in me, even when I didn't think I did. Thank you to the incredible and indefatigable team at Dey Street Books, including: Lynn Grady, Benjamin Steinberg, Heidi Richter, Kelly Rudolph, Kendra Newton, and Sean Newcott, all of whom guided me through this process.

Editing comes in all forms, but for this book, the most helpful editors were trusted friends and confidants who insisted that I listen to the sound of my own voice. Thank you, Nathalie Wade, Christina Bellantoni, Paola Mendoza, Maria Gabriela Pacheco, Diana Espitia, Arvind Murthy, Mony Ruiz-Velasco, David Buchalter, Lara Drasin, Alejandra Campoverdi, Luisa Heredia, and Marcia Davis. A very special shout-out to Barbara Feinman Todd, whom I met nearly a decade ago when I helped teach a multimedia journalism class at Georgetown University. After I read her book, *Pretend I'm Not Here,* I knew she would be the ideal sounding board (and therapist) as I dug deeper into my psyche. This book was written in Airbnbs, in hotel rooms, and in the spare bedrooms of Elise Haas and Cristela Alonzo. I finished it while sleeping and working in Nicole Ponseca's living room. Thank you, Bob Haas, for telling me that it was okay to take time off to think and write this book.

I am a product of three families: the family I was born into, the family of friends and mentors I found here in America, and the family that makes up Define American. Many members of my families are recognized throughout this book, and you can meet my entire Define American family, including our board of trustees and advisory board, at defineameri can.com/team. My eternal thanks to the earliest supporters and champions of Define American, particularly Barbara Picower of the JPB Foundation, Taryn Higashi of Unbound Philanthropy, Cathy Cha of the Evelyn and Walter Haas Jr. Fund, and Liz Simons of the Heising-Simons Foundation. Thank you to Ryan Eller for your leadership and the grace in which you exhibit it. Thank you, Jonathan Yu, for putting up with me at all times.

Thank you to Lola, my beloved grandmother, for your love.

Reading Group Guide

1. What drew you to read *Dear America*? Had you heard of the author, Jose Antonio Vargas, before reading the book? If so, what was your impression of him before reading the book? Why do you think the author gave the book this particular title? Who is he addressing? What is the significance of the fingerprint on the front cover?

2. America once prided itself on being "a nation of immigrants." How has the national view of immigrants and immigration changed since the founding of the nation, and especially over the past fifty years, since the passage of the 1965 Immigration and Nationality Act? Do you believe that America is (still) a nation of immigrants? Why or why not?

3. What does it mean to be an American? What makes an individual a citizen? Who should get to choose who is and isn't allowed to become an American and live here? In learning about Jose, is he any less an American than those who are born here? Why or why not?

4. Jose opens *Dear America* with the words "I do not know where I will be when you read this book." What emotion did you experience when you read that sentence?

5. Why doesn't Jose think of himself as an activist? Would you consider writing—perhaps even reading—*Dear America* to be activism?

6. Jose explains that the book is not about immigration, but about homelessness. How does he separate the two? What makes a place a home for someone? What does it mean not to have a home? Have you gone through something like this before? If not, do you think you could endure living in limbo—choosing not to put down roots, moving from place to place, fearing that you will be arrested?

7. What does it take to survive as an undocumented person in the United States today? How has living a lie and hiding shaped the person Jose is and the profession he chose to pursue? How did he mask his status from those who did not know his secret before he came out as undocumented?

8. Jose touches on race in the book. Why is race a charged issue for Americans? Why do many Americans feel the need to identify foremost by race? How do race, nationality, and immigration influence one other?

9. How many generations of your family were born in the United States? Do you know when the first generation of your family arrived in America and where they came from? Do you know any immigrants today?

10. Why do many Americans seem to dislike immigrants, both those who hold green cards and those who are naturalized—and especially those who are undocumented like Jose and the other Dreamers? Do you think America's immigration laws are adequate? Or do they need to be changed? Do you know what changes the Trump administration is seeking to our current laws? Or what they are currently doing under executive action?

11. What do you think would happen if we deported all undocumented immigrants—around 11 million people, the size of the population of Ohio—in the country? How would we find them and "round them up"? Does the use of language like "rounding up" people remind you of any other time or place in history? If so, how?

12. Should Dreamers, who have never known any country but the United States, be deported, or be allowed a path to citizenship? Why?

13. What did you discover about Jose Antonio Vargas from reading *Dear America*? Did anything you read surprise or shock you? What does his story say about the plight of the millions of other undocumented men, women, and children in the United States today?

14. How has reading *Dear America* affected your opinion about immigration, migration, citizenship, and being an American? What are some common misconceptions the author dispels about "illegal" immigrants? Did you know that the process of citizenship was as difficult as it is?

15. *Dear America* explores how the media often distorts the lives of everyday immigrants. How do your interactions with immigrants compare to what you see in the media? Is America as divided about immigrants as the media says? What is it like in your community? #factsmatter

16. *Dear America* delves into how anti-immigrant hate groups have successfully used mainstream media to legitimize hate speech. How can you combat dehumanizing and inaccurate phrases like "illegal immigrant" or "alien"? What other words do you see the media using to describe immigrants that are dehumanizing? #wordsmatter

17. In *Dear America*, the author explores how the media often refers to and quotes organizations—which the Southern Poverty Law Center has designated as hate groups—in order to substantiate the government's anti-immigrant policies. How can you help hold journalists accountable when quoting sources? Does the media have a responsibility to its audience to avoid citing hate groups in their coverage of immigration? Why or why not? #sourcesmatter

About the Author

Jose Antonio Vargas, a journalist and filmmaker, is the founder and CEO of the nonprofit Define American. His work has appeared internationally in *Time*, as well as in the *San Francisco Chronicle*, *The New Yorker*, and the *Washington Post*, where he won a Pulitzer Prize as part of a reporting team. In 2014, he received the Freedom to Write Award from PEN Center USA. He directed the documentary feature *Documented* and MTV special *White People*, which was nominated for an Emmy Award. An elementary school named after him will open in his hometown of Mountain View, California, in 2019.

More info on joseantoniovargas.com